THE OTHER SIDE
OF THE WORLD

"I have reached the conclusion that the natural world can only be understood in depth as a series of images symbolizing concepts."

OWEN BARFIELD
The Rediscovery of Meaning

THE OTHER SIDE OF THE WORLD

ESSAYS AND STORIES ON MIND AND NATURE

William H. Eddy

2001

The jacket map and interior halftones are
from a 1985 print by Auron Ashley Inc. of
Yonkers, New York, taken from a Dutch atlas
published in 1640 by Johannes Jansonnius
and Henricus Hondius of Amsterdam.

1. Mind/nature relationship
2. Environmental philosophy
3. Environmental perception

ISBN 0-9708951-0-0
LCCN 2001 126237

Printed in the United States of America at
The Stinehour Press, Lunenburg, Vermont.

Distributed by Enfield Publishing and
Distribution, Enfield, N.H. 03748

Table of Contents

ACKNOWLEDGEMENTS

I would like to acknowledge that two of the longer African tales, "The Man with the Sun in His Hand" and "A Garden Far Away", first appeared (1976 and 1977 respectively) in *Blackwood's Magazine* published in Edinburgh, Scotland. That remarkable magazine of stories and essays began its life in April of 1817 and was published every month without exception for over 163 years. The final issue came out in December of 1980. In its long and honorable history, it published pieces by some of the greatest writers in the English language: Wordsworth, Dickens, Thackeray, Hardy, Hawthorne, Emerson, Kipling, and Poe, just to mention a very few. It was a magazine unique in both quality and continuity. I consider it a privilege to have been a very small part of that great and now vanished tradition.

The story "Of Ships, Giraffes, and Unicorns" first appeared in Vermont Public Radio's magazine *North by Northeast*, December 1986, Vol. 1 #8.

I would also like to acknowledge the keen eye and thoughtful criticism of my editor, Susan Kashanski. She not only edited the book, but she undertook the multifarious tasks associated with publishing, designing, marketing, and distribution. It was her encouragement and belief that there was a readership for the book that lit the not infrequent darkness prior to its birth.

The book itself is evidence of the design and printing skills of The Stinehour Press in Lunenburg, Vermont. Avanda Peters understood from our first meeting what it was we wanted to produce, and she translated it all step by thoughtful step into reality. The handsome end product is very much in keeping with the outstanding and well-deserved reputation of this unusual company.

Introduction

Because a collection of essays or poems often covers an extended period of time in an author's life, it might be said that it offers a mirror to reflect the writer's image. I prefer, however, to think of these essays as forming a window rather than a mirror — one through which the reader may see familiar things, albeit from an unfamiliar perspective. Thus the reader may become conscious not so much of the writer's mind as of the reader's own view of things.

If the essayist or poet is skillful, then the reading becomes an encounter with ourself and our own habits of looking. Thoughtful readers bring with them a complex of often unconscious perceptions and assumptions about the world, and it is on these that a writer is totally dependent.

Most of these essays were first written as commentaries for Vermont Public Radio spanning a period of about four years. It was the warm and thoughtful response of listeners to those commentaries that prompted me to collect them in essay form. Others of the essays I first presented as ideas in lectures, or at conferences, while still others have appeared in various publications.

One of the pleasures of writing commentaries for radio is the discipline of dealing with often complex ideas in a time frame of approximately four and a half minutes. Some listeners found the ideas to be so concentrated that they wrote to ask for copies they could read. When one is listening to a reading, there is no opportunity to determine the pace of participation, so I hope that the written form here provides the interested reader the chance to enter more fully into the ideas and also to make a choice about the order in which they are read. Although the essays have been given an order, that order is not essential to their reading or meaning. They are best approached with the expectation that each is a whole in itself.

Some of the essays are anecdotal, describing my experiences over 35–40 years working on a variety of environmental concerns among unusual peoples in remote parts of the world — with the Rendille and Maasai tribes in East Africa, and with various peoples in India, Nepal, Thailand, Sri Lanka, and Tibet. Others of the essays are concerned with the history of Western thought and the evolution of that special way of looking at the world that we call "scientific". Still others are concerned with the mind's evolving relationship with nature over time, and how that, in turn, has shaped our perception of nature's own evolution.

I think it requires only a modest change in the habits of

our thinking to recognize that prior to the existence in the world of something like human consciousness, nature could not have had a solely objective existence. A world of "objects" exists only in relation to a "subjective" percipient. Where no subjective world exists, it is meaningless to speak of an objective world. Subject and object are mutually dependent; each provides the environment from which the other may be perceived — not unlike the relationship implicit in such polarities as "up" and "down" or "front" and "back". So with the evolution of human consciousness, structured by language, the world became polarized, albeit gradually, into the "it" that appears to be outside of me and the "I" that appears to be inside. Thus the advent of human consciousness and the correlative growth of language created for the first time what might be described as both an "outside" to nature as well as an "inside". Despite the tenacity of popular belief to the contrary, neither can exist without the other.

If there is any theme or concern that these essays share in common, it is, in various guises, this one — that the mind is, in reality, the other side of the world.

I believe the implications of this idea are critical to our survival as a species.

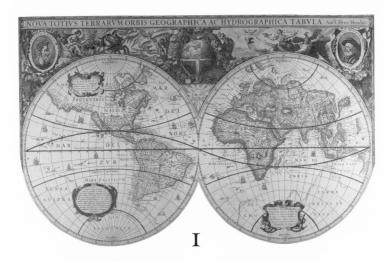

I

Other People, Other Places

We begin with stories of some of the people and experiences that have been part of my forty years of environmental work — often in remote places. In retrospect, I can see how they led me to question many of the habits of my thinking and many of the stereotypes through which I viewed the world.

The Rendille

The Northern Frontier of Kenya is a vast area of dry country that reaches to the borders of Somalia, Ethiopia, and Sudan. It is a storybook landscape — remote and essentially roadless — whose horizon is ringed by distant mountains that sometimes turn to gold just before the sun sets.

It is a land of old volcanoes whose massive lava flows lie staggered on top of one another like the steps of giant stairs. In places, the land is strewn with rounded lava rocks that look like missiles from some forgotten Stone Age war among the giants.

Flying over the country in a light plane, one sees signs of the nomadic desert people — the Rendille, the Gabbra, and Boran — perhaps a circular cluster of huts made of goatskins tied to skeletons of wood. In the center, a barren circle of dung marks the night enclosure made of thorn bush to protect the livestock from theft or from marauding lions.

The Rendille, the Gabba, and Boran are different tribes with different languages, and although these differences are what define them, the tribes are similar enough to be competitive. Thus they are intermittently at war over theft of livestock and of women. But from the air, their nomadic way of life seems much the same. They struggle to survive in a world that we would find impossible, but, since it *is* their world, they see it differently — so differently that neither we nor they could easily understand.

They worship each their gods. They mourn the death of children. They laugh at stories told. The ritual flirtation between the beaded girls and spear-thin warriors is carried on the night wind in the sounds of dancing and of song, themes that run as counterpoint to the other ceremonies that mark their birth and puberty, their marriage, and their death.

In short, they are a people who retain some clarity about who they are.

I went to the Northern Frontier of Kenya to work with the Rendille tribe as part of a UNESCO project to study the spread of desert. My job was to determine first whether portable video equipment could stand the rigors of that environment, and second to see whether video could be used to help the people better understand their own involvement in the spread of desert.

To carry into that harsh and simple desert world such complex and delicate equipment as the cameras, recorders, and monitors dramatized for me how separate were our worlds and how different was the view from each.

Sometimes I think the only way we must grow aware of

our environment is from the very context of a different one. It is almost as though we cannot see except in differences.

One night I had a showing for some Rendille of a television tape I'd made for them. The showing took place in a tiny one-room building erected by a Catholic mission as a future schoolroom for Rendille children. After my audience had left, and as my Rendille interpreter, Kareo, and I packed up all the pieces of equipment, I tried to imagine how the Rendille would explain to each other those moving images and sounds of themselves, their camels, and their lives.

How could they understand a cathode-ray tube with its electron gun that converts intensities of light into electric pulses that travel down a wire to another tube that changes electricity back again to light, and writes that light in colored dots to make up pictures of their camels on a screen at the rate of thirty images a second?

As Kareo and I emerged from the little classroom and out into the velvet desert night, it was by contrast like being launched into space. Our tiny planet seemed adrift under an immensity of sky whose crystal dome had shattered into countless brilliant particles. As we walked toward the Land Rover, I looked up at the stars, my mind filled with images of other solar systems in other galaxies, of distances measured by the speed of light, of quasars and black holes, and I thought that such a vast and complex vision of the universe would be no easier to explain to these people than a cathode ray tube or an electron beam.

5

I turned then to Kareo. "When the Rendille look at the night sky, Kareo, what do they see up there?"

"Oh," he replied, "we see the eyes of God. Why? What do your people see?"

I had no way of answering the question.

The Maasai

For many Americans, the most familiar of the African warrior pastoralists are probably the Maasai of Kenya and Tanzania. We may not know that the particular individual is a Maasai or even that he comes from East Africa, but we have seen the pictures so often that he has come to represent the prototype of the romanticized image of the African male: tall, thin, wrapped in an ochre-colored cloak or *shuka*, and leaning on a seven-foot spear. Often the pictures show him standing on only one leg—the other bent into an acute angle with the foot hooked behind the unbent knee. At a distance he appears as a flamingo wading at the water's edge.

So despite the rapid changes that are transforming the face of Africa as it rushes to embrace the best and worst of 21st-century Western culture, there is still something about the Maasai that, for us, links them to the timeless natural world of Africa. And, of course, there is something in us, too, that wishes to perpetuate this rapidly fading image.

Among the Maasai, there seems to be a kind of calculated arrogance, a regal aloofness, especially among the young warriors, or *morani*, with their dangling braids of ochered hair and lean bodies glistening with red clay — a kind of easy disdain for all the comforts and clutter of possessions that to their eyes make the Western tourists seem both funny and grotesque. They think nothing of loping across 50 miles of trackless bush in a single day. They do it just for fun.

They envy no one, and those Maasai who do leave their culture for other worlds often return to that way of life they value most. And although we have romanticized these people beyond reality, there are grains of truth, in fact, that help to keep the romance very much alive.

I remember a story about a Maasai told to me by Ernest Hemingway's son, Pat, when we lived as neighbors in East Africa.

Pat had been a professional hunter for many years, and when, for personal reasons, he decided to wind up his career, he took one last safari with his mother and a couple who had been old friends of his father. They were not there to hunt, except, perhaps, for food. They were interested primarily in seeing and photographing the wildlife.

Pat had decided to go on safari into an area that lay south of the famous Serengeti plains in Tanzania. It covered hundreds of roadless square miles on the map — an area that he had hunted in before but which he did not know well. On their way in they had picked up a hitchhiker, a middle-aged Maasai, his red *shuka* flapping about thin legs, copper ornaments dangling from each elongated earlobe, and on his wrists, two carved bracelets of ivory. He carried with him a symbol of authority among older Maasai, a knobbed fighting stick known as a *rungu*. Pat talked with him in Swahili and discovered that he knew the area intimately. So it wasn't long before a bargain had been struck whereby the Maasai would go with them as a guide.

Very early one morning toward the end of the safari, Pat went off with the couple to try to photograph a leopard. His mother had decided to remain in camp to write some letters and to read. As she sat at the small folding table outside her tent, she saw that their Maasai guide, Kerogwe, had also remained behind. There was nothing unusual about this, but it was the first time that both of them had been alone in camp together. She was curious about the Maasai. They seemed so different from the Bantu-speaking people of East Africa. She knew nothing of their strange tonal language known as Maa, and her Swahili was limited to some greetings and a few basic household words, useless for the kinds of questions she wanted to ask. She knew that some Maasai did go to mission schools, and she wondered if perhaps Kerogwe might have done so and learned a bit of English. It wasn't long before she had the opportunity to find out. Approaching him somewhat tentatively, she spoke slowly and deliberately.

"Kerogwe," she asked, "you speak English?"

"Oh, yes, madam," he replied. "I speak English fluently."

She hesitated. "My son doesn't know that, does he?"

"I don't believe so," Kerogwe answered. "But his Swahili is really quite good, so we haven't needed to resort to English."

"Did you learn to speak English in mission school?" she asked.

"Only the rudiments, madam," he said. "You see I spent three years as a high-speed telegraph operator in the British navy."

A Lost African Chief

There are not many times I have felt it necessary to call the police. Once, in the middle of the night in the heart of New York City, it seemed the only choice I had left. Over the phone I explained. "Yes, I've lost an African chief," I said. "I believe he arrived at Kennedy airport this afternoon from Tanzania several hours ahead of schedule. He hasn't checked into the hotel. It's his first time in America, and I thought if he did get lost he might call the police."

My mistake had been to mention an African chief. But that's what Chief Adam was — Adam Sapi — paramount chief of the Wahehe tribe, speaker of Tanzania's House of Parliament, and Chairman of the Board of the Tanzania National Parks.

In 1962, African chiefs weren't very common in this country, even in New York City, and so when I said that I had lost one, whoever was on the other end of the line at precinct headquarters apparently visualized a tall black man, draped in spotted skins, with a large bone thrust sideways through a topknot of hair, maybe two front teeth neatly filed to sharp points, and carrying a seven-foot spear. And here was this lost apparition stalking the sidewalks of 43rd Street at midnight looking for his hotel. It's interesting to think how times have changed. Today such a figure on the streets of New York would probably go unnoticed.

The next morning Chief Adam phoned me. He had arrived earlier than scheduled and had gone to a small hotel frequented by Tanzanian delegates to the United Nations.

I haven't seen Chief Adam in years. I am sure he is no longer alive. But in those days, he was a tall, distinguished-looking gentleman with graying hair and mustache. He was always impeccably dressed, most often in a dark-gray pinstriped suit, and he carried himself and spoke with a kind of gentle authority, as one long accustomed to the leadership of what he called "my people".

The Wahehe tribe come from the central highlands of Tanzania where, in the early part of the 20th century, they formed a core of resistance to German colonial rule. Instead of obeying the order to come to Dar es Salaam with other tribal leaders to acknowledge German authority, the Chief of the Wahehe, a man called Mkwawa, gathered his people together and built a mud wall ten feet high and nine miles in circumference, behind which he prepared to withstand a German attack. Then, Mkwawa's medicine men, believing they could turn the enemies' bullets to water, laid a powerful curse on the Germans.

The German expeditionary force with 20th-century

artillery and very real bullets attacked Mkwawa's defenses, breached the mud wall, and forced Mkwawa's people to surrender. To avoid the indignity of capture, Mkwawa shot himself in the head.

I visited the Wahehe in the early 1960s, and while there I was invited by my host to see the memorial erected to Mkwawa by his people. We drove through the fertile land past innumerable small and well-kept farms, and came to a stop under a huge and ancient fig tree where Wahehe tribal problems had been discussed and resolved for generations. A short walk brought us to a small brick building with a slate roof — a kind of Georgian anachronism in the midst of thatched huts. As we entered, I noticed a damp smell of a building not often used. In the center of the single room stood a shiny black pedestal on top of which was a glass case. Inside it was a human skull with a clearly defined hole in one side. On the walls of the room was a series of large black and white photographs, which my host proceeded to explain.

Apparently, following Mkwawa's suicide and the Wahehe surrender, the severed head of the chief was sent back to Germany, as an anthropological artifact, a trophy of war, who knows? And there it was lost.

After Germany's defeat in World War I, Tanganyika, as it was then called, was mandated to Britain as a trust territory, first under the League of Nations, and then later, following World War II, under the United Nations.

Just after World War II, Lord Twining, the British

administrator of Tanganyika, began a search for Mkwawa's skull. Perhaps the search was made easier because the allies occupied Germany, but, at any rate, the skull was eventually discovered in the anthropological museum in Bremen.

Then in a formal ceremony in the 1940s, Lord Twining, on behalf of the British government, returned Mkwawa's skull to the Wahehe people. And there, in the last of the pictures, standing next to Lord Twining, I saw a younger version of my gray-haired host, Adam Sapi, my lost African chief, holding in his hands the long-lost skull of his grandfather.

Maps and Territories

In September of 1970, I was filming in southern Tunisia on
the edge of that part of the Sahara known as the Great
Eastern Desert. I had been commissioned by the U.S.
National Park Service to produce a film and to write a book
on the earth's environment. Together they were to be the
gifts from our Park Service to the delegates of nearly 100
nations who would be attending the Second World
Conference on National Parks to be held at Grand Teton
Park in September of 1972. So the conference was still two
years away, and a long road lay ahead that would take me
filming in the deserts of Tunisia, the high mountains of
Ethiopia, to Kenya, Japan, Thailand, and Europe.

All this was yet to come when I found myself in a small
oasis village called Douz in Tunisia on the edge of 60,000
square miles of sand dunes and rock. (It was this same dramatic desert that was featured so prominently in the
Academy Award-winning film *The English Patient*.)

I had gone there with two colleagues to shoot a sequence
on the camel caravans organized by the oasis dwellers to
gather firewood from the desert. Ten or fifteen men with as

many camels would set off into the desert for as long as three weeks at a time to collect wood from the dessicated forests that had been inundated by the inexorable northward movement of the sand.

Because their purpose was to bring back as much firewood as possible, they carried with them only the barest minimum of food and water.

There was no margin for error — an accident or navigational blunder would have been disastrous. For days at a time, endless crescent-shaped dunes stretched to the horizon, the sand itself as fine as talcum powder. The wind that slept at night awakened each morning with the coming of the sun to reshape the landscape in a matter of hours until it was unrecognizable. The best of maps would have been useless. And, thus, because there were no reliable landmarks and because of the fierce heat during the day, the men preferred to travel at night, navigating solely by the stars.

Setting off for three weeks by camel into the vast desert must be one of the great journeys left on earth. For me, it gives new meaning to the words "endangered species" — in this case a species of ancient knowledge that, when gone, will represent a loss perhaps as great as that of a rare plant or animal.

I have, since those days in Tunisia, become increasingly aware of our human world as sharing many of the elements of that natural world of constantly shifting sands, in which no earthly map has meaning. Ours is a time of such rapid change that when we pause to wonder at our direction, whether as individuals or as nations, whatever maps we may have no longer seem to fit the territory in which we are traveling. And today, few people look to the heavens for guidance. Many have become disastrously lost, and the list is growing. We hear their names each day — Bosnia, Iraq, Kosavo, Rwanda, Afghanistan, Somalia, North Korea.

Perhaps we might best describe such a world by saying that the events of the present are shaping a future that no longer looks as it once did from the past. And the old maps, those truths that we once perceived as absolute, no longer seem to work. Our certainty of what the world is like withers in the harsh light of reality.

But the greatest danger that comes from using maps that are no longer accurate is the tendency of the traveler to blame the territory for the inaccuracies rather than the map itself. It is the age-old conflict that occurs when the ideal stumbles upon the real.

Sometimes I envy those camel men of the desert who have the stars to guide them. They travel in darkness over wind-shaped sands with a certainty that we no longer know. For us today, however, the guides we need are not outside us, distant and remote like stars. They can only be found inside among the precious natural resources of the mind and heart, in the power of imagination, and the human will. Perhaps our greatest hope is in knowing that, like the stars, it is darkness that calls forth their light.

The Dhami at Labar

In the Himalayan country of Nepal, near its eastern border with Sikkim, lies what is reputed to be the deepest river valley in the world. The Arun River, which originates in the high plateau country of Tibet, descends through Nepal from north to south forming the valley between Mt. Everest to the west and Kanchenjunga to the east. High in the northern reaches of that valley where the river swirls its wildest, atop one of the labyrinthian folds of land made by the Arun river and its countless tributaries, there lies a small and beautiful meadow. It is called Labar by the local people, and it is they who come up from the lower villages after the snowmelt to graze their cattle and goats — and they know the place. In March, the small meadow is filled with the fragrance of viburnum, which grows along its edge. One end of the meadow perches dizzyingly thousands of feet above the river. There, years before, the entire mountainside slid into the valley below, leaving the still-open wound of exposed soil, boulders, and tumbled trees. When asked the date and cause of that landslide, a local herder will tell you that it took place many years before, and that it was brought about by an event in a village several days' journey from the meadow. For the landslide occurred, it seems, on the very day that a Hindu girl and a Mohammedan boy were married.

In the center of the meadow there is a small, clear pool fed by an underground spring. One day in February of 1973, a scientist from an American zoological expedition collected a frog from the pool. Shortly afterward it began to rain — an event made more unusual by the fact that the monsoon season was still four months away. The rain continued for two days, and at the nearby base camp the porters became surly and restless, as did the Sherpa assistants.

Hadn't Dr. Burns Sahib collected a frog from the pool just before the rain began? Was some ritual of restitution now necessary to appease the restless spirit of the place? Perhaps the head Sherpa, Nima Chotar, should speak with the expedition sahibs. And as it continued to rain, that is precisely what Nima Chotar did.

Now the expedition sahibs were not unlike you and me. They were Americans; they knew the difference between superstition and science — which is to say that their education and culture had provided them with a particular set of premises by which they explained and interpreted what they called the real world. Thus they knew there could be no relationship between the admittedly unusual weather and the taking of a frog for scientific study. But they agreed that something should be done, if only to raise the gloomy spirits of the porters and the Sherpas.

So at Nima Chotar's suggestion, a runner was sent off to Lumdumsa to bring back a *dhami* — what we would call a witch doctor or a shaman, if you will — an employable intermediary between humans and the spirit world. Nima Chotar believed that a skillful *dhami* would set things right. He estimated it would take the runner two days to reach Lumdumsa village, and, if all went well, another three days or so for the return climb. On the fifth day, exactly as predicted, the runner returned in the rain with the *dhami*. They reported that the weather in Lumdumsa had been clear.

The *dhami* apparently knew the earlier story of Labar meadow and its landslide. When shown the area, he went immediately to the pool from which the frog had been taken. At the edge, he built a small fire and prepared to cook some rice. From an old leather pouch he took various bits of bone and teeth, along with some pieces of dried skin covered with long brown hair. He placed them carefully in front of him.

In a strange high voice, cracked and piercing, he sang over the pool and the cooking rice. Then he scattered the steaming grains over the water, where they fell among the raindrops. Afterward he sat silently as in a trance, staring at nothing visible.

Then suddenly he was on his feet, putting out the fire, and packing away his things. He led the small procession of porters, Sherpas, and sahibs back to basecamp. There the sahibs paid him for his work, and then, shouldering his few belongings, he set off in the rain for Lumdumsa.

The next morning dawned bright and clear. Everyone was pleased — especially the sahibs, whose decision it had been to send for the *dhami*. They knew of course that there could be no connection at all between the mumblings of an old man and the weather's clearing. But they agreed that the *dhami*'s coming had been good for morale.

Towers of Silence

Seeing the film *Gandhi* when it was first released some years
ago reminded me of how little our American culture pre-
pares us for the experience of India. Our senses have
become tuned to a world that by comparison seems rather
bland and hygienic. India overwhelms us with the strange
textures of its multiplicity of peoples and languages. India
is poverty-stricken and opulent. It is splendid and filthy. It
is a model of religious tolerance with a history of hatred
and violence. India is so old that we think of it as timeless,
and it is so young that nearly half its one billion people are
only fifteen years old or younger.

Nowhere do these irreconcilable contrasts stand out
more vividly than in India's large cities. Bombay is such a
place. Lying a third of the way down India's west coast,
Bombay is actually an island separated from the mainland
by a winding and heavily polluted creek. At the southern
end of this island city, two arms of land reach into the
Arabian Sea to form what is known as Back Bay. From the
northernmost arm rises Malabar Hill, containing one of

Bombay's wealthiest residential areas. Looking east and north from the hill, one has fine views of the city, especially in the early morning before the heat haze — before the air is thick with the noise and exhaust of countless trucks and crowded buses, and before the sky is grayed by the pall of smoke from the huge refineries in the north.

With its ultra-modern skyline, its rooftop gardens and expensive penthouses, Bombay is the movie-making and entertainment capital of India, complete with a wealthy international jet-set. It houses as well a considerable portion of all the factories in India and produces 40% of all the textiles. It is estimated that at night almost 4 million of its more than 10 million people sleep on the sidewalks.

A visitor to Bombay should make a point of seeing the hanging gardens on Malabar Hill. It is hard to imagine a contrast greater than that between the din and chaos of the city below and the serenity and beauty of those gardens.

Just past the gardens, one comes to a high wall behind which there is yet another park, but this is not open to the public. It is a sacred place called the Towers of Silence, and it is here that the Parsees dispose of their dead.

Thirteen hundred years ago, the Parsees fled to western India from their home in ancient Persia to escape religious persecution by the invading Muslims. Their beliefs go back some 600 years before the time of Christ to the teachings of a Persian named Zoroaster, or Zarathustra, as the Greeks called him. Zoroaster believed that the world was divided between the forces of good and those of evil — between the power of light in contest with that of darkness. At the head of the good was Ahura Mazda, whose purity of spirit was revealed in the natural elements of earth, air, fire, and water. Contamination of these was considered a contamination of God. So careful were the Parsees of the natural environment that they refused even to farm the land for fear of hurting earth. Instead, they went into commerce and today are often found among the leaders of the Indian business community.

Even now, however, the Parsees neither bury their dead in the ground nor do they allow cremation. They believe that bodies of the dead would contaminate not only the earth but the flames of the fire as well. Instead they place the corpse atop a 20-foot-high circular tower, and while the family sits quietly in the beautiful gardens nearby, the body is consumed by vultures. In time the bleached bones of the dead are swept down a central hole in the tower.

But there is a strange irony in all this. For there is evidence that the increasing industrial pollution of Bombay's air is destroying the habitat of the vultures. As their numbers dwindle, their important work at the Towers of Silence is slowly being taken over by a more resilient species of large hawk called the pariah kite. But the feeding habits of the kite are quite different from those of the vulture. Instead of consuming their food in one location as the vultures do, the kites tend to carry off pieces to various parts of the city, sometimes dropping them on the streets below. The town fathers of Bombay consider this an intolerable form of pollution, representing on the one hand a disrespect for the dead and on the other an affront to the living. It is not difficult to share their view.

The irony is that the pollution that is destroying the vultures comes from factories owned by the Parsees — the very people for whom the contamination of earth, and air, and fire, and water is considered a contamination of God.

Plane Tales from the Hills

Some years ago I worked on a project in India that took me to Kanha National Park. Kanha is one of India's great natural areas filled with animals whose names are almost completely unfamiliar to us — names like gaur, sambhar, chital, barasingha, sloth bear, and musk deer. But this is true of much of India. There are many things there that we would find unfamiliar.

To get to Kanha by air from New Delhi, I had to make a series of short hops southward on Indian airlines — from Delhi to Gwalior, to Bhopal, to Jabalpur — and then a four-hour drive to park headquarters.

The aircraft from Delhi was a crowded, high-wing, twin-engine affair with double seats on each side of the aisle. I swung my small bag onto the overhead rack and took an aisle seat next to a crisp-looking Indian army officer. The noise of the engines on takeoff obliterated any chance for conversation, so it was not until we were airborne that I had the opportunity to talk with him.

I would have said he was in his early fifties. He had a

small gray mustache and closely trimmed graying hair, and he looked physically very fit. He had made a career of the army and was currently in charge of a heavy equipment construction crew in the Corps of Engineers.

In response to my questions, he explained that he was on his way to visit his wife and family on leave from a project far off in northeastern India. There he was in charge of building a road in the dense jungle to provide access to remote villages. As I remember, he said it was somewhere north of the Brahmaputra River in the Indian state of Assam. Most Westerners know little about this huge northeastern corner of India that on the map lies both above and beyond the country of Bangladesh.

It is a melting pot of diverse and ancient people: Aryan, Dravidian, Mongolian, and Tibeto-Burmese.

There are literally dozens of different tribal groups strung together in loose federations of so-called Union Territories and small states with names like Meghalaya, Manipur, Nagaland, and Arunachal Pradesh.

My traveling companion described the area where he worked as so remote and difficult to reach that the heavy equipment had to be flown in in slings beneath big military helicopters and lowered into the jungle, while the laborers made the long trek in by foot. He said that the local forest people had had little contact with the modern world, and he spoke of the army's having recently encountered a small community further north in Arunachal Pradesh where the people lived in caves and ate their food uncooked because they had not yet discovered the use of fire. What he said seemed hard to believe, but the most remarkable part of his story was yet to come.

After the first bulldozer operators had arrived at the camps and had gone to work clearing the huge boulders and trees from the future road bed, he said the drivers began to report seeing small dark-skinned people who appeared and disappeared like phantoms among the trees. They would apparently watch the work for a while and then vanish. They did not seem to pose any threat to the workers, but the drivers felt uneasy.

And then he described how very early one morning before the dozer operators had begun work, a procession of men and women came in single file out of the forest. They were carrying garlands of fresh flowers and carved wooden bowls filled with flower blossoms and fresh fruit.

In what apparently was a ritual ceremony of some kind, they approached the earth-moving machines and placed the garlands of flowers over the vertical mufflers and on the cushioned seats. Then they placed the bowls of fruit on top of the engine cowlings. They remained completely silent. They made no effort to communicate with anyone. And then they walked single file back into the jungle.

The officer said that each morning for several days the ritual offering was repeated. The procession would again withdraw, and from the cover of the jungle they would watch the work begin.

As the days passed and work on the road bed progressed, the people of the jungle no longer appeared.

The officer was obviously moved by and curious about the strange behavior of these people. He respected their innocent belief that the bulldozers were living creatures of which they stood in awe. And he also realized that all the ordinary, routine early morning procedures performed by the drivers prior to their work had been carefully observed from the forest as ritual acts: the filling of the tanks with diesel fuel, the tightening of a loose nut with a wrench, and finally the mounting of the seat and the turning of a key. This was the final act of a daily ritual necessary to awaken with a deep rumble the power of the beast.

Such an experience leaves one without appropriate words to give expression to its meaning. Perhaps one can only paraphrase something that Shakespeare once said under very different circumstances: "There are more things in heaven and earth . . . than are dreamt of in our philosophy."

Canyon de Chelly

In early May of 1992, I spent a week at Canyon de Chelly in northeastern Arizona.

Canyon de Chelly is part of the Navajo Indian reservation, but it is also a National Monument. In other words, it is part of our National Park Service, whose role there is essentially as custodian of an important natural, historic, and cultural site.

Each year, tens of thousands of tourists visit the canyon. The uniformed park service personnel they meet are, for the most part, Navahos themselves — some of whom are direct descendants of the first Navaho families to enter the canyon in the early 1700s.

Canyon de Chelly was occupied by a succession of early peoples whose dwellings and artifacts can be traced back well over a thousand years before the arrival of the Navaho. These early peoples are sometimes referred to collectively as the Anasazi. The Navaho simply call them the "old people". And, although they were not related, the Navaho consider the caves in which the old people lived, along with their stone buildings and various artifacts, as sacred.

Each year, Navahos who work at the National Monument at Canyon de Chelly hold a training program for seasonally employed staff who will interpret for visitors the history and culture of the area. I had been invited to talk to the trainees and to share in their training experience.

The first two days we spent in classroom sessions looking at the Navaho culture against the background of the canyon's geology, natural history, and archeology.

Then we spent three days on foot in the canyon itself. With us on our walk were a few older Navahos — each a specialist in some aspect of Navaho traditions — in the medicinal use of plants, in tribal history, in folklore, in religion. It was like passing through a time warp into a vanished world. We walked in places the tourist does not see. We were shown caves high on the side of the canyon walls where no archeologist has ever dug, some of the caves accessible only by rope from the canyon's rim, others only by toeholds carved in the vertical walls.

Passing through layers of time, we first came upon a recently discarded saddle beginning its long decay in the hot sun. Nearby, lying on its side, was a derelict horse-drawn hay baler with the painted date of 1918 still visible. The saddle and the baler lay close to the base of the canyon wall. High on that rock face, higher than a human could easily reach, was a faded row of painted images of animals and people. They are believed to have been painted in the early 1700s.

To the left of the baler and saddle there was a shallow cave in the sandstone wall. Amidst the rubble on the cave floor pieces of pottery were visible, preserved in the hushed and timeless silence that permeates the canyon — a silence made deeper by the distant voice of a raven calling.

As the afternoon sun descended, the light changed. The canyon walls glowed burnt orange, then bronze, then ochre, and the shadows on the floor and walls of the canyon grew like pieces of the coming night. It was the same light I had seen in north Africa reflected from the sandstone ruins of ancient Roman cities — the presence of the vanished people made more intense by their deserted houses and broken possessions — and always the same silence.

At night before we went to sleep under the stars, a Navaho storyteller recounted one of the many tales of first man and first woman. As all such tales, it began with the words "once upon a time", and we were led once again through that familiar doorway into timelessness, and to the story of how children were first given to the human race.

To return from that world to the one of airports and rental cars is not an altogether negative experience. Because for a short moment, one is privileged to be poised between two worlds, occupying neither. And briefly one's perception of both is heightened.

What sets those worlds apart for me is the way in which time is measured in each.

The Navahos live immersed in slower rhythms — in time

that's measured by a shadow's change as on a sundial, or by falling sand as in an hourglass. In such measurements one may read at a single view what has been, what is, and what is yet to come.

In our world the measurement of time is digital, on clocks that have lost the simple humanness of face and hands, on clocks that speak only of what is now, in which there is no past that's visible and the future, too, is unseen.

In the Eye of the Beholder

A picture, it has been said, is worth a thousand words.
The problem is that it has been said so often that we no
longer pay attention to its meaning. But if we consider
the statement, we find that it suggests that information
and even understanding are conveyed by picture faster
and more comprehensively than by written or spoken language. Although we have come to accept this as a truism
in our culture, my own experience with remote peoples in
Africa and Asia suggests that there the statement has little
validity.

My work with the Rendille tribe in northern Kenya in
the 1980s was a small part of a massive project undertaken
by UNESCO – the United Nations Educational, Scientific
and Cultural Organization. They were there to determine
the causes of desert spread. My task was to develop ways to
introduce the preliterate, camel-raising Rendille to a better
understanding of their own role in the spread of the desert.

On one of several trips I made to the area my son, Cam,
then 26, was with me, and since we were living in a

Rendille village, we had a perfect opportunity to test their reaction to pictures.

The Polaroid Corporation had provided us with special 35mm film along with the developing equipment necessary to produce color slides in a matter of minutes.

With this film, Cam documented a variety of objects that formed an integral part of Rendille life — a bead necklace, a spear, the communal water tank, and baskets made of woven grass for carrying water. Then, using these pictures, he ran a test with a selected group of Rendille.

Years earlier while making films for African audiences in Tanzania and Uganda, I had believed, along others working in that field, that pictures could revolutionize the education of people for whom the written word was inaccessible. I assumed that the visual skills of people who couldn't read were the same as those who could. And then I met Alan Holmes.

Alan was British. Three decades of his seventy years had been spent with the Flying Doctors' Service in Kenya, bringing medical care to remote clinics in the African bush. For years, Holmes had been asking patients waiting in the clinics to interpret the meaning of a series of simple drawings that he had put together. Over the years, he had amassed quantities of data that he graciously shared with me. Before he died, Holmes became a legend of sorts, and his work in Africa formed the reference point for similar studies in perception in many parts of the world. Holmes's remarkable conclusion was that among people who can neither read nor write there is often a high percentage who cannot easily adapt to the traditions by which Western art depicts the three dimensions of space on a flat surface. Photographs were for him simply an extension of those traditions.

Certainly the Rendille responses to Cam's photographs of familiar objects were in keeping with what Holmes had concluded. The people chosen for the test were of both sexes and of all ages. The pattern of response was that younger males and females recognized more of the pictures than did older people. The recognition of pictures by the few boys and girls who had learned to read at the local mission school was almost 100%. With older people, we had no way of knowing whether poor eyesight was a limiting factor, but it was interesting to note that all the Rendille tested were able to recognize a picture of a spear and a sword regardless of the viewer's age, gender, or education.

It was, however, the exceptions that were most interesting.

The photograph of a pair of leather sandals propped against a log was seen by the owner and maker of the sandals as a warthog. The only shop in the village, a rectangular structure of cement blocks, was interpreted by one elderly gentleman as a giant wearing a green belt. And a woven grass container for gathering camel's milk was seen independently by different viewers as an eclipse of the moon, a rhinoceros, a house, and the sun behind some clouds.

What this and other studies suggest to me is that what

we see and what we know cannot be separated. We perceive what we expect to perceive, and the sensory data that reach the eyes are translated by mind into meaning and then projected outward to reappear as part of what we, in our particular group or culture, call the real world.

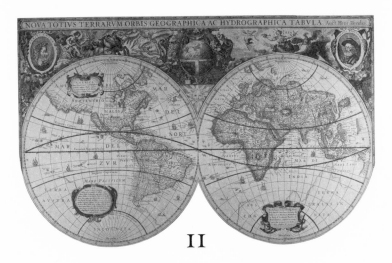

II

Beyond the Familiar

Looking at something from a particular perspective is really a matter of looking at one environment of thought from another. A word such as *medieval* can only have definition as perceived from a different environment of thought such as that described by a word like *renaissance*. Since the former way of seeing can be perceived only by comparison with the latter, we might construct a law of perception that says that it is impossible to perceive any environment except from the context of another.

Each of the essays included in this section offers an environment of thought from which another less familiar perspective may more clearly be seen.

Kenge and the Buffalo

I remember some years ago talking with my friend Colin Turnbull about his work with the Mbuti pygmies of the Ituri forest. The Ituri lies in the easternmost part of what used to be known as the Belgian Congo and later became the African nation of Zaire. Not long ago, as you may remember, that same nation changed its name once again to Congo. Turnbull lived in the Ituri forest for several years in the early 1950s, and he describes those experiences in his marvelously warm and human book *The Forest People*.

To encounter the very real differences in perception of another culture, especially when that culture is as different from ours as the pygmies' is, can have a startling impact on us. It makes us aware, often for the first time, that there is much in our own way of looking of which we are completely unconscious.

So I was especially interested in Turnbull's description of a journey he took by Land Rover with his pygmy friend Kenge to look at wildlife in a national park many miles east of the Ituri forest. Kenge had never before been outside of the forest; he had never seen any land that was not densely covered with trees. And so entering the open savannah and rolling grassland of eastern Zaire forced on him an entirely new perspective — that of seeing familiar things at an unfamiliar distance.

At one point in their journey, Turnbull stopped the Land Rover at the top of a hill, where they could see in every direction. There, well over a mile away, Turnbull pointed out to Kenge a large herd of cape buffalo. Kenge shook his head. He was perfectly clear they were not buffalo. "What kind of insects are those?" he asked. For the buffalo that Kenge knew were those of the forest — large animals seen only at close range. From this new perspective, the buffalo became a quite different reality — perhaps as the earth might appear when viewed for the first time from the moon — perhaps as youth might appear as seen from the distance of old age. A shift in perspective, whether in time or space, can greatly affect the reality we see.

In another part of Africa, I had a similar encounter with the problem of perspective. It happened while I was standing on the rim of an extinct volcanic crater.

The Ngurdoto crater in northern Tanzania is part of a small and lovely national park. In a way, the crater represents a distillation of the essence of East Africa as it used to be. One can see the impala and the elephant, the bushbuck and the giraffe as specks upon the crater floor. It is almost as though one were viewing them through reversed binoculars, looking backward down the long corridor of time to a world before the emergence of man.

Measured on the African scale of things, the crater is not very large — perhaps a mile or so across its floor. And the highest elevation along its forested rim is about 6,000 feet.

Standing on the crater's edge in the early morning after a rain, one often has a fine view of Mt. Kilimanjaro, some twenty or thirty miles to the east. There is no higher mountain in the whole of Africa; its summit rises nearly 20,000 feet above the Indian Ocean. Having stood both on the crater's edge and on the mountain's summit, I don't know if one can say which view is more beautiful. Each offers a very different perspective. From the rim of the Ngurdoto crater, Mt. Kilimanjaro seems rather small and the crater itself tends to dominate the view. But then this is true of so much of human perspective. Whatever lies in the immediate vicinity of our concern draws the lion's share of our attention. And that is perhaps as it should be.

But I know that from the perspective of the summit of Kilimanjaro, the Ngurdoto crater simply does not exist.

Maybe it is important from time to time to change our perspective on whatever lies closest to us — to threaten just a little everything that is familiar, by viewing those things from a distance. Such a shift in perspective may help us to overcome what appears to be our dangerous tendency to make insects out of buffalo or mountains out of molehills.

What Did the World Look Like Before There Was Anyone Here?

What do you suppose the world looked like before there was anyone here to know that it was this world? There must have been millions and even billions of years before there was anything like a mind that was conscious of its surroundings as we are. So what did the world look like then?

I suppose we should probably call it a nonsense question, but at the same time we all know a great many people who would be perfectly clear about the answer. And what would they say? Well, perhaps something like this:

Oh, yes, I've been to the Museum of Natural History in New York and seen all those marvelous dioramas of prehistoric times. You know the ones I mean, where Brontosaurus — actually I think his name's been changed recently to Apatosaurus — is up to his stomach in a huge swamp happily munching on a mass of dripping vegetation. On the distant shoreline you can see Triceratops and Tyrannosaurus locked in terrible combat, and behind them a forest of tree ferns covers the land as it rises

44

toward a distant volcano. Thunder clouds have formed above the volcano's plume of smoke and ash, complete with the flickering of hidden lightning, and in the distance a rainbow arcs across the sky. Everything seems so realistic that it's almost like being there. You can almost hear the sound of the thunder. I bet that's pretty much what the world looked like before there was anyone here.

Doesn't it seem strange that we never question such a perspective? For quite clearly those dioramas are the projections onto the past of the present view of the sciences. It is a view that would be shared only by Western-educated people in the last 200 years — which does, indeed, seem a brief moment in the long history of the human effort to find meaning in experience. For meaning changes, and if the past has anything to teach us, it is that our present set of lenses will offer only a distorted image of the world to the people of future generations.

What we share in common with each other as well as with people from the past and the future is that none of us is aware of wearing any lenses at all. Our vision appears to us as both clear and undistorted, and we call it the truth. It was Werner Heisenberg, one of the pioneers of quantum physics, who once commented: "What we see is not nature itself, but nature exposed to our particular form of questioning."

My point simply is to suggest that our particular form of questioning has led us at the beginning of the 21st century to believe that there is something called the objective real world that exists independently of us and which existed for millions and even billions of years before we appeared.

Thus our science is concerned not only with the important task of prediction, as when we attempt to foretell the impact of global warming on future crop production on the basis of what we know at present, but it is also concerned with what might be called postdiction, as when we describe the causes for events in the past on the basis of what we know in the present. Postdiction is concerned with the interpretation of events that occurred long before there were any minds in existence that looked at the world in our particular way.

The projection onto the past of our present way of looking seems to occur almost unconsciously. We're all familiar, for instance, with the name used by astrophysicists to describe that awesome initial moment of cosmic creation. They call it the "Big Bang". What we may be less aware of is that such a description inescapably suggests the presence of a listener — someone not unlike ourselves — someone to hear the sound. For how could there have been a "Big Bang", or a "Big Light", or a "Great Heat", without someone present whose senses or instruments were capable of recording the experience in those terms?

So when we're asked what the world looked like before there was anyone here, it is at best a meaningless question.

How any world looks depends on someone who is doing the looking and for whom that world *means* something. Five hundred years ago when someone looked under a "hood", he would have expected, perhaps, to find a monk. Lifting a "hood" today one would expect, and would find, a very different reality.

Galileo — Truth and Consequences

On Monday, November 2nd, 1992, the following news item appeared as a one-inch column on the front page of the *Wall Street Journal*. It read: "The Roman Catholic Church conceded after 359 years that it was wrong to have condemned Galileo for asserting that the earth orbited the sun. Pope John Paul II on Saturday accepted the findings of a panel that studied the case."

That piece of news probably didn't ripple the waters for very many readers that day. Not just because they were so caught up in anticipation of the next day's presidential election, but because we have come to consider history as an area of concern in which by definition everything is out of date. And for us what is out of date is increasingly irrelevant to the here and now. This is a very different view of history from the one that asserts that the "past is prologue".

It is from this latter view of history that I would say Galileo was prologue to far more than he could have imagined, and furthermore it had little to do with the notion that the earth went round the sun. To understand what in fact he did do, we need to separate myth from history.

In myth, Galileo is often portrayed as the heroic underdog battling against the institutional power and ignorance of the Catholic Church. We have to set this against the recorded personality of a man who was arrogant, grasping, and particularly ungenerous toward the astronomical observations of others.

In 1623, the prominent Jesuit scientist Horatio Grassi published a paper in which he offered an explanation for three comets that had appeared in European skies five years earlier. Reading Grassi's essay, Galileo was angered that his own name had not been mentioned as the authority on comets. Apparently there still exists a copy of Galileo's response to Grassi written in Galileo's own hand. But instead of signing his own name to this response, Galileo signed the name of one of his students. Thus he could safely attack Grassi for not recognizing the important contribution to the study of comets made by one Galileo Galilei.

Another myth suggests that Galileo was punished by the Church because, without their permission, he made public his discovery that the sun was the center of the universe. But Galileo discovered no such thing. A sun-centered universe had been seriously proposed by Aristarchos of Samos some 1900 years before Galileo. But more importantly, ninety years before Galileo's trial, a canon of the Catholic

Church in Poland by the name of Koppernighk, more familiar to us by his Latin name Copernicus, had published his description of a sun-centered universe and had been urged to do so by the Catholic Church.

How could it be that the Church would urge Copernicus to publish his ideas about the universe, and then later on threaten Galileo with torture if he did not renounce those same ideas?

Copernicus had created a model to explain the various motions of the planets and stars. But it was only a model. Certainly the Church perceived it that way when, in 1616, they told Galileo and others that it was permissible to teach Copernicus as hypothesis—that is, as a model to preserve the appearances of things in the sky. But no man, they said, could be certain how God achieved the same ends. That would be a presumption that was beyond human knowledge.

But Galileo was not convinced.

In a now famous letter to a critic who had questioned whether his observations of the sky were in conflict with religious teachings, Galileo had responded by borrowing a quote from the Vatican librarian who had said, "The Bible tells us how to go to Heaven but not how the heavens go." Galileo was looking for the truth about nature in a very different direction from the Bible. He was suggesting that an individual observer could, through his own sense experience, interpreted and structured by the mind, arrive at hypotheses that were not simply models of reality but were in fact the way things really are.

What Galileo believed he had discovered was that the Copernican model was not simply a hypothesis but that it was true.

The British author C. S. Lewis in his little book *The Discarded Image* says of Galileo: "The real reason why Copernicus raised no ripple and Galileo raised a storm may be that whereas one offered a new supposal about celestial motion the other insisted on treating this supposal as fact. If so," he concludes, "the real revolution consisted not in a new theory of the heavens but 'a new theory about the nature of theory.'"

It is this perspective that has so dramatically shaped our relation to nature ever since. The Church had clearly perceived the threat that Galileo posed. And while they might force him under threat of torture to renounce Copernicus as truth, they were unable to put a blindfold on this new way of looking at everything. Today we refer to it as the "scientific revolution".

Let's Change the Subject

In the previous essay, I wrote that it was in the year 1623 that Galileo published a scathing attack on a prominent Jesuit astronomer who had had the temerity to suggest an explanation for comets that was different from Galileo's. And there, buried amidst all his anger and vituperation, Galileo quietly introduced one of the most important ideas in modern thought. He described, for the first time that I am aware of, the distinction between those qualities that are inherently part of an object and those that are contributed by the mind and senses of an observer.

Let's take the example of a brown leather briefcase.

Now Galileo would have said that our experience of the briefcase involved two sets of qualities. What he called primary qualities were those he believed to be inherent in the briefcase itself — ones that existed independently of us as observers. They would have included the briefcase's shape, solidity, position in space, and its number — in this case, one — and its motion, if any.

What he called the secondary qualities were colors,

odors, tastes, and sounds. For these existed, he said, only when a human observer was present.

He wrote of the distinction this way, "I think if ears, tongues and noses were removed, shapes and numbers and motions would remain but not odors or tastes or sounds. The latter are nothing more than names when separated from living beings."

What Galileo was describing were the early stages of that remarkable separation that was beginning to take place in the 17th century between the human as subject and the world as object — a separation that was to grow rapidly over the next 300 years. It was the creation of this dual world of subject and object that lay at the heart of what we call the scientific revolution.

One of the most interesting ways to trace such revolutions in thought is to consider how the meaning of words like "subject" and "subjective" have changed over that same period of time. That great record of the history of Western thought, *The Oxford English Dictionary*, tells us that prior to the 17th century the word "subject" meant "the essence or reality of a thing", and "subjective" meant "real or essential". This meaning still lingers today when we speak of students taking different "subjects" in college, or when we speak of the "subject" of a sentence.

But within 100 years of Galileo the word "subject" had begun to reveal a subtle change in meaning. By the mid-18th century, the *O.E.D.* describes it as that which is "pecu-

liar to an individual subject or his mental operations" —
that which is "personal" or "individual". And by the late
19th century, the change was complete. By then "subjective"
had come to mean "existing in the mind only, without anything real to correspond with it — illusory or fanciful".

But soon after this gulf had been opened between the
imaginary and the real, between the subjective and the
objective, then another extraordinary change began to take
place.

Early 20th-century physicists had inherited from such
thinkers as Galileo, Newton, Descartes, Bacon, and many
others, a "real" world of solid objects that existed whether
or not an observer was present. But it wasn't long before
discoveries in relativity and particle physics led scientists to
consider that the position, motion, and solidity of things
were, in fact, qualities that had meaning *only* if an observer
were present.

It is interesting to note how tenaciously our belief per-
sists in the existence of an external world that is solid,
shaped, and in motion independently of us. Entire sciences
have been created based on that perception — geology, for
one, and evolution, for another — sciences that depict the
world as it was for millions and even billions of years before
humans appeared, but whose description, we can now perhaps begin to understand, is meaningless except in terms of
human sense experience as interpreted by a Western-educated observer from the 21st century.

So in our time, Galileo's careful division between the properties of objects and the properties of mind has indeed become blurred. Today it appears that the only remaining property attributable to objects themselves is number. The rest of reality seems to be up to us.

Perhaps we might conclude from this that the only way to really change the world is to change the subject.

The Great Reversal

Gravity is such a familiar part of our experience that we seldom think about it. But its existence serves to remind us that we tend to remain unconscious of those elements in our environment for which there are no exceptions. It makes one wonder what other everyday phenomena surround us of which we are unaware.

The effects of that force that we call gravity have probably been around since the beginning of things. But as a universal "law of nature", gravity has been with us only a little over 300 years.

It was in 1687 that Sir Isaac Newton published his great work on the mathematics of the forces that hold the earth and moon together and at the same time keep them apart. He called the one force gravity, adopting it as a metaphor from the already familiar medieval word "gravity", which itself had come earlier from the Latin word "gravis".

Prior to Newton, the word gravity simply described the heaviness of things. One spoke of a pregnant woman as being "gravid". But gravity was also used for a kind of heaviness that was not only physical, as when one spoke of a "grave" situation or of the "gravity" of an important issue.

In medieval times, people would have said that a stone thrown in the air returned to earth not because of a force called gravity but because earth was where stones belonged.

And the word "belong" is particularly appropriate because it carries with it some of the emotional overtones of longing and desire that medieval people would have metaphorically attributed to any object seeking to return to its home. The physical body of the dead person belonged in the earth, while the soul yearned to travel upward seeking its natural home in heaven.

Implicit in such a view was the medieval sense of "being" with which it was believed the entire universe was animated. Mind and intelligence were to be found everywhere – in the stars and planets and even in the air – while gravity was strictly a local property of the things of earth and man.

Newton was to change all this, but not by intention.

Building on Galileo's work on the trajectory of cannon balls and the acceleration of falling objects, and building, too, on the work of Johannes Kepler who believed that magnetism might explain how planets moved in orbit around the sun, Newton created a new synthesis with his idea of a law of universal gravity. His was uniquely a mathematical description – one that explained and predicted the flight of cannon balls, the behavior of falling stones, or the orbit of the moon around the earth.

We have forgotten how difficult it was for Newton to accept the idea of an invisible but physical force that acted everywhere across empty space. Writing to a friend of his, he said that the idea "that gravity should be innate, inherent and essential to matter, so that one body may act upon another at a distance through a vacuum, without the mediation of anything else . . . is to me so great an absurdity, that I believe no man who has in philosophical matters a competent faculty of thinking, can ever fall into it."

So Newton was never certain about the nature of gravity. On the one hand, in describing it as a purely physical force, he explained that it traveled through space by means of an invisible substance called the ether that propagated gravity much as sound travels in air. On the other hand, he apparently believed that gravity might be a measurable yet unexplainable expression of God's power. In the notes at the end of his great work he concluded: "The supremely elegant structure of the solar system cannot have arisen except through the device and power of an intelligent being."

Such concerns with whether gravity was a material force or a manifestation of the creator's mind were in time forgotten. What remained for later scientists were Newton's remarkable mathematics and the resulting predictability they gave to the motions of bodies in space.

After Newton, a subtle change occurred in the way the whole of nature was seen. It was a change that we find difficult to perceive because our own thinking is itself a product of that change. The medieval idea of gravity that was limited to the things of earth became a physical property of the entire universe. And the idea of mind that had so permeated the medieval universe became relegated only to the heads of humans on earth. We today have yet to fully understand the implications of that great reversal. As with the subject of gravity, despite its importance to our lives, we seldom think about it.

The Missing Link

The Aberdare National Park is a 230-square-mile area of
moorland and mountainous forest that is part of the central
highlands in the East African country of Kenya. While the
park is justly famous for its wildlife, it is perhaps better
known to Western tourists for its Treetops Hotel. This
remarkable structure, complete with bedrooms and bal-
conies, restaurant and bar, is perched some twenty feet in
the air on the topless trunks of giant trees overlooking a
nearby water hole and artificial saltlick. From this tree-
borne perch, visitors may watch in comfort and security as
a Noah's ark collection of wildlife gathers in the early
morning and evening, or even under floodlights late into
the night.

There have always been elephant at Treetops, often with
their young. Not many these days, however, with the
poaching. But the cape buffalo are still there, the warthogs,
the monkeys, and baboons, many different species of
gazelle, sometimes giraffe. Rhinoceros once were common,
but today there are fewer than two hundred in the whole of

Kenya. Rarely one sees leopard. If you're especially lucky, you may catch a glimpse of that beautiful forest gazelle, the bongo. It is a large animal, maybe four feet at the shoulder, and its bright chestnut coat slashed by white vertical stripes mimics the play of sunlight with shadow in the high bamboo forests of the Aberdare mountains.

It was while visiting Treetops Hotel on February 5th in 1952 that a twenty-five-year-old English woman first heard the news of her father's death and learned that, as a result, she had become Elizabeth II, Queen of England.

Some years later on June 20th, 1969, a quite different event took place at Treetops. Kenya's vice-president, visiting dignitaries, and members of the press had gathered for the unveiling of a plaque to commemorate the addition of a new wing to that unusual hotel.

Another witness to that small ceremony held on the hotel rooftop was a female baboon. Having quietly ascended the side of the building during one of the speeches, she had swung herself up onto the wooden railing that skirted the flat roof on which we had gathered, and there she sat quietly some ten or twelve feet from us. From time to time during the ceremony, I caught myself looking at her and wondering whether her claim to be there was not at least equal to mine. Perhaps hers was the greater claim because this, after all, was her country and her home, and so naturally she had an interest in being there. She stayed through the several speeches, the words of praise for the architect's ingenuity, and finally for the moment of the unveiling itself. Not unlike us, she glanced occasionally at the covered trays of food and glasses of refreshment that would be served once the ceremony was over. Her manners were impeccable, and her patience competed favorably with ours.

After the ceremony, as we ate and drank and talked of Kenya and its tourist potential, its wildlife and parks, several people spoke to her; others offered a piece of cake or a small sandwich — much as one would to any guest. Having partaken of the refreshments, she simply sat and watched us, drawn perhaps by the sounds and gestures of our conversation, perhaps by the clink of ice in glasses, or by the pleasant sounds of mandibles munching sandwiches.

Although mindful of the dangers of an anthropomorphic view of other creatures, I am aware of the equally dangerous distortions of a view that is essentially anthropocentric. Man's image of himself as superior to other creatures might well cause us to wonder what our response will be to that historic first encounter with intelligent life from another solar system.

Meeting with an intelligence superior to ours not only in knowledge but in understanding, we might find ourselves, overnight as it were, classified by them as simply another planet of the apes. What is more disturbing, perhaps, is our tendency to measure every creature we encounter on a descending scale from man. One wonders whether this might prevent us from recognizing a superior intelligence even if we were to meet with one.

It was, I believe, Konrad Lorenz, the father of the study of animal behavior, who once said, "The missing link between the ape and the human being — is man." Difficult as it may be for us to accept such a perspective, it does at least keep open the possibility that as a species we still have something to become.

De Docta Ignorantia

Some time ago, I was invited to speak to a group of elementary school teachers who were beginning a three-week training program at the University of Vermont. They were part of a project being undertaken by University faculty from the departments of chemistry, physics, and geology designed to help teachers of the very young to introduce their students to the sciences.

I began by saying that I always found it difficult to talk to a group of people whom I did not know and who did not know me. It meant, I told them, that we shared no common frame of reference. For example, I said, the words I am using may be familiar to all of us but for each of us their meanings may be different. Consider a word like "nature". To what does it refer? Trees and sky, lions, wolves, and bats? What about dragons and unicorns? Well, they aren't part of nature, you say; they only exist in the imagination. Is the human imagination a part of nature? What about cities and computers? No, they're man-made. Well, what about a vegetable garden? Is that man-made, too?

Does nature itself have any environment? I asked. In other words, is there anything that's *not* contained in nature? If there is nothing that *isn't* nature, then how can we identify what it is — as different from something else? Usually a container like a box is clearly separate from the things it contains.

These are not easy questions to resolve, I said, but they do illustrate that we could talk about nature for a long time before we realized that we each might be talking about something quite different.

So, in short, I said, "I don't know what you *know*, and I don't know what you *don't* know. But then, of course, neither do you."

It seems such an obvious fact that we can't be aware of what we are not aware of. But how difficult it is to understand. As one writer has said, our consciousness is like a flashlight in a dark room. To ask it to reveal something on which there is no light shining is meaningless. So our ignorance remains in the dark and we remain unconscious of it. As we learn more, our consciousness casts its light on objects in the room that we hadn't seen before, and, gradually we may become dimly aware not only that our ignorance is vast but that the room itself is infinite.

One man who saw this problem so clearly and expressed it so well was Nicholas of Cusa. Cusa was the Latinized name of the tiny German village of Kues where he was born in 1401.

Nicholas was a man for all seasons. He attended the universities of Heidelberg, Rome, Padua, and Cologne. He became a bishop in the Catholic Church. He was fascinated by astronomy and mathematics and pursued the study of botany and optics. It was Nicholas who concluded that the universe, like God, "had a circumference that was nowhere and a center that was everywhere". In 1440 he wrote of these ideas in a little book titled *De Docta Ignorantia*.

A translation of that Latin title might be "on learned ignorance", or it might be "on learn-ed ignorance". For Nicholas of Cusa, it apparently meant both.

The ignorance that grows from increased knowledge is an ignorance that we become aware of only as we learn. The brilliant physicist who, after a lifetime of research, has become aware of the limits of his own knowledge has learned his own ignorance, and, insofar as he is aware of it, his may be a "learn-ed" ignorance as well — in the sense that a "learn-ed" person is wise, something more than just well educated.

Such ignorance may well be worth striving for. It is quite different than the common garden variety of ignorance — the unlearned type that simply comes from not knowing. We see it in the arrogance of politicians, or in that tendency toward certainty in so many middle-aged males. It is revealed in the swagger of the eighteen-year-old soldier with the automatic rifle. We hear it in the cry that says that freedom and "doing what you want" are synonymous. It was best said on a bumper sticker I saw recently. It read:

"The best substitute for experience is being sixteen." It reminded me that one reason for the slow pace of human progress may be that each generation must learn the particular dimensions of its own ignorance. That is the daunting task of teachers.

Piece of Mind

On December 6th, 1993, a short essay appeared on the editorial page of the *Wall Street Journal*. It was written by Stephen Meyer, a professor of history and the philosophy of science at Whitworth College in Spokane, Washington.

Meyer describes events that took place the previous fall at San Francisco State University when a professor of biology by the name of Dean Kenyon was prohibited by his department chairman from teaching courses in introductory biology.

Professor Kenyon, who holds a Ph.D. in biophysics from Stanford University, is described by Stephen Meyer as "an authority on chemical evolutionary theory." In a book he co-authored in 1969 called *Biochemical Predestination*, Professor Kenyon explained the process by which living cells might have emerged from the chemicals present on the early earth. Since then Kenyon's research has led him to conclude that no such evolution could have taken place without the "guidance" of some form of "intelligence". In short, he has come to believe that something like mind had a role in shaping life.

The chairman of the biology department removed Kenyon from his courses because he said that Kenyon was teaching religion.

Stephen Meyer in his essay comments, "The simplistic labeling of Mr. Kenyon's statements as 'religion' and the strictly materialistic view as 'scientific', seems entirely unwarranted. Biology texts," he continues, "routinely recapitulate Darwinian arguments against intelligent design. Yet if arguments *against* intelligent design are philosophically neutral and strictly scientific, why are Mr. Kenyon's arguments *for* intelligent design inherently unscientific and religiously charged?"

The issue here seems to me to be very different from the arguments for or against the teaching of Biblical Creationism in biology classrooms. At the root of the problem lies our definition of what we mean by the word "mind". It is only from the habit of our own thinking that we automatically assume that to suggest mind as a shaping force in nature must imply something mystical, religious, or supernatural.

In 1987, a remarkable book appeared titled *The Margins of Reality*. It was subtitled *The Role of Consciousness in the Physical World*. Written by Drs. Robert Jahn and Brenda Dunne, it provides a detailed record of experiments undertaken since 1979 at the School of Engineering and Applied Science at Princeton University.

The research by Jahn and Dunne into the role of mind in

the physical world grew out of a question posed by one of Jahn's graduate students. As micro-electronic circuits become smaller and more delicate, is it possible, she asked, that the functioning of instruments using such circuitry could be measurably affected by the thought process of their users? Jahn believed that the answer to this question could have important practical implications for the use of computers, air traffic control systems, and even missile guidance devices.

One part of their carefully controlled and thoroughly documented work involved the construction of a testing device called a Random Event Generator. An electric current is passed through an electronic device called a noise diode from which is emitted a measurable electronic pattern of binary pluses and minuses. By the use of a sampling device, the diode's random output can be measured hundreds of times every second. The resulting data provide an electronic version of "flipping a coin" thousands of times every minute with the binary pluses equivalent to heads and the minuses equivalent to tails. Thus, it is possible to graph the pattern of output of any particular diode. Once that pattern has been established, then a lab worker is asked to attempt by thought alone to increase or decrease the diode's "normal" distribution of pluses or minuses.

The results of literally millions of tests involving many different participants for nearly two decades reveal that the mind can, indeed, measurably influence the results. And whether that mind is in the same room as the Random Event Generator or whether it is thousands of miles away makes no difference to the results.

In the conclusion to their book, Jahn and Dunne suggest that the method they have developed at Princeton might be applied to measure the influence of thought on the behavior and even the structure of living organisms such as algae, sperm, and bacteria. One recent report I read states that approximately 100 papers already exist describing successful experiments in this area.

One cannot help but ask whether we may be standing on the threshold of a major scientific revolution — one in which "mind" may come to be seen as an invisible, universal, and yet measurable force, of which our own minds are part — a force that may have played as important a role in the structuring of the universe as that other recently discovered invisible, universal, yet measurable force we call gravity. The implications of such an idea are enormous. Who knows? Perhaps someday Professor Kenyon of San Francisco State University will be welcomed back to the classroom to teach a very different way of looking at evolution.

The Sea

It is many years ago that I remember reading the story of a young Englishman named Peter Bird, who, by himself, rowed a small boat across the Pacific Ocean from California to Australia — a distance of some 8,000 miles. One cannot help but wonder about the impact of such an experience. Certainly it must have provided him with a very different perspective not only of the sea and the land but of himself — a perspective that most of us can only imagine but never really share with him. In many ways, that experience forced on him a remoteness and a sense of isolation greater than that experienced by the astronauts who have gone to the moon. He was on his own in a way that they were not.

Humans have always been attracted to the sea. It may be that its power and size, together with its changing moods and mystery, create for us a perfect reflection of the human mind itself. It has lured us to explore its depths, to chart its unknown regions. And as it fascinates and beckons, there is also something about the sea that makes us fear that we may venture out too far or in too deep — and not return.

It is difficult for those who live along the seacoasts of the world to realize how many millions of others have never seen an ocean — have never stood alone on an empty stretch of rocky coast or sand beach watching the huge waves from the open sea. Such an experience provides a view of our planet quite different from any other on earth.

One's first and strongest impression of the sea is the smell of salt and rotting seaweed cast up by the tide. It is not for everyone a pleasant experience. The smell is powerful and old — the odor of the body of life as it has existed since the earliest creatures first smelled the air for meaning.

A thoughtful person standing at the ocean's edge, as the great waves curl and thunder, is aware of standing also on the shores of time — of looking out across the past into the dim origins not only of our own creation but of every form of life on earth.

Listening to the surf, we may become aware of other rhythms, too — of the strong, slow beat of our own heart pumping the salt fluids of our blood in echo to the pounding waves. And even though we may not understand such things, some part of us will sense the ancient kinship of our body's blood and tears and sweat with the great salt body of the sea.

Such an experience does not involve the human mind alone, for that part of us attracted to the sea is older than our reason and older than the shapes that human thought may take. We remember dabbling at the water's edge as children, searching in the salt pools left by the falling tide for signs of life, turning over a submerged rock and finding beneath it a starfish, perhaps a crab, a broken shell — believing always, as we searched, in the possibility of finding something new, or more precisely, something very, very old.

Beneath the surface of our consciousness lies hidden perhaps the desire to uncover some evidence, some specific proof for that ancient journey by which life first crawled from the sea to make its home on land. Like a memory that flickers dimly at the edges of the mind, we see in our imagination some nameless ancestor on unformed feet dragging itself along the water's edge, gasping the strange air — one of a long procession of unfamiliar creatures emerging slowly from the sea — crossing the warm mud flats, clinging to the rock cliffs, gradually gaining a foothold on the land, burying eggs in the sand, and struggling to survive in the new environment of sun and air. And we know that this is the way that we have come, and we know, too, that for us there is no return now to the sea.

So Peter Bird and his 8,000-mile journey alone across the Pacific stands for me as a kind of metaphor for that other long journey through space and time undertaken by the human animal on its way to becoming who we are.

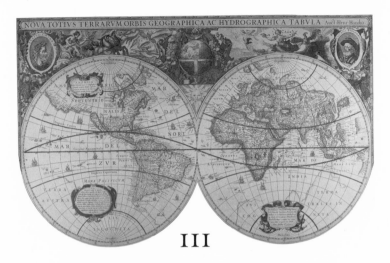

III

"Words, Words, Words . . ."

Readers familiar with Shakespeare's *Hamlet* will recognize these words as the young prince's response to Polonius's bumbling question, "What do you read, my Lord?"

Confused by Hamlet's answer, Polonius continues, "What is the matter, my Lord?"

"Between who?" Hamlet asks.

"I mean the matter that you read, my Lord."

The delight we take in the many-faceted play of words is one of the great pleasures of being human. Our species' remarkable capacity to derive new meaning by making verbal comparisons between things that have no necessary connection tells the fascinating history of the evolution of human consciousness itself. These four essays venture only a short distance into the vast landscape of language and metaphor.

"In the beginning . . ."

I find it interesting how seldom we wonder at the age or origin of the spoken word. There is something special about human speech that separates us from all other creatures. For only we can talk in metaphors and only we can leap the barriers of time to speak of things long past or of events that may or may not be in times to come.

How long ago did speech begin, and how are we to trace its origins? The earliest records of our written languages are not much older than some 7,000 years. The difficulty of our quest for the origin of spoken words is that speech leaves nothing for the fossil record.

We do know that our capacity for speech required more than just the will to talk. Over millions of years, specific areas of the brain evolved to provide the trellis of language on which our thoughts could grow. Is there something in the physical brain itself that would enable us to find when speech began?

The outer surface of the living brain in fact imprints itself upon the inner surface of the skull, and so if liquid latex is poured into an empty skull and then allowed to set, one is able to remove a rubber impress of the outer surface of the brain that used to be. In this way, Ralph Holloway of Columbia University believes he has discovered in a nearly two-million-year-old skull of one of our earliest relatives, *Homo habilis*, the imprint of what he thinks may be Broca's area — one of the three regions of the brain's left side that are crucial to forming spoken thoughts.

Does this mean that *Homo habilis* could speak? Perhaps, but gorillas and chimpanzees are said to possess a rudimentary Broca's area as well. So only by conjecture could we attribute speech to *Homo habilis*.

Where else then can we search for the origins of speech? Is there anything preserved from our earliest behavior that reveals a mind that worked in metaphors — that found new meaning by naming ways that different things were similar? For making metaphors is another name for making words.

The earliest and, I think, most provocative evidence for the existence of speech comes from the great cave at Shanidar in the Zagros mountains of Iraq, some 250 miles north of present-day Baghdad. Beginning in the late 1950s, excavations by Ralph Solecki, then of Columbia University, revealed that the cave had been occupied continually by humans for 100,000 years. Even today the local Kurdish herdsmen seek the shelter of the cave in winter for themselves and their flocks.

Solecki uncovered the graves of some nine Neandertals at

Shanidar dating from different periods over thousands of years. The burial known simply as Shanidar 4 was discovered in 1960. It was the skeleton of a male, and so difficult was it to excavate bit by bit that Solecki covered the bones and their matrix of soil and stones in plaster of Paris and removed the entire complex.

Two years later at the Museum of Man in Paris, Arlette Leroi-Gourhan began to study the soil around the skeleton. She found it contained the pollen of a remarkable diversity of ancient flowers. Among them were cornflowers, grape hyacinth, a yarrow, yellow groundsel, rose mallow, and hollyhock. So great was the concentration of pollen that for it to have been carried there by the random motion of the wind seemed most unlikely. In writing of the flowers Solecki said, "They were not accidently introduced into the grave. Some person or persons once ranged the mountains collecting these flowers one by one." He dated the burial at more than 60,000 years before the present.

The human capacity for articulate speech had probably evolved much earlier — just when, we cannot know for certain. But in the flower burial at Shanidar we are clearly present near the dawn of humanness — a humanness that coupled the consciousness of death with flowers in such a way that as metaphor they speak to us across 600 centuries to express the hope for some alternative to death and the promise of another season of renewal and rebirth.

We tend to think of metaphor as the product only of

sophisticated minds much later in our social evolution. We think it but a trick of language — a brittle device of literary art. But is it possible that just the opposite is true — that metaphor was the first and oldest of our verbal tools through which we learned to speak the world into existence and ourselves to consciousness? It has been said "In the beginning was the word . . .". I wonder if at Shanidar it was the word for flowers.

Metaphor

In another essay I used the word metaphor to describe the way in which new meaning is introduced to language. It is a process in which a relationship is made in a speaker's mind between two apparently separate sense experiences, as when someone says, "The ship plowed the waves."

Most often we think of metaphor in connection with poetry — as when Shakespeare in the opening lines of one of his sonnets compares the succession of waves on a beach with the passage of time in human life. "Like as the waves make toward the pebbled shore / so do our minutes hasten to their end." But while such metaphors are simple and clear, we tend to remain unaware of how metaphor pervades all of language, and, more importantly, of its tremendous power to influence how we think.

The word metaphor, itself, can be traced back to two Greek terms: "meta" meaning across or beyond — and a second term "pherein", which was the Greek verb "to carry" or "bear". The "ph" sound in Greek became an "f" in Latin and later showed up in English in a word like "ferry". A ferry boat is one designed to "carry or bear" passengers. This same idea occurs in the "fer" of an English word like "transfer", which means to carry something across. A metaphor, then, carries across or transfers meaning from one sense experience to another. "He ran like the wind." Thus it makes possible entirely new ways of seeing and interpreting experience – something that poets have been especially good at for a long time. It is a peculiarly human capacity of which most of us remain completely unconscious.

Imagine, if you will, that you had lived in the country outside ancient Rome. There, a road from the south intersected one from the west and another from the east. Over time, at this intersection of three roads, you saw a small market grow up – a few stalls that sold cloth or spices, various foods, cooking utensils, or cheap jewelry. Thus the intersection became a stopping place for people traveling through, and in time a small village may even have appeared. Then, as more time passed, you began hearing a new word – one that was used to sum up the characteristics of such intersections, all of which seemed to involve a similar kind of activity – one that wasn't world shaking – one that didn't shape the events of the empire as great battles or as decisions of the Roman senate did. It was a special kind of activity that required a human mind to identify and to name. The new word was made up from the Latin for

"three roads". The first syllable was "tri" — meaning
three — as in English triangle or tricycle. And the second
syllable was the Latin for roads — "via". Together they
entered our language as the familiar English word "trivia".

Thus a new meaning had been created in which the three
roads of the intersection had become a metaphor for the
most common and daily of human experiences, those
which we speak of today as being "trivial".

Many other metaphors are much more difficult to see. In
English, for instance, we attribute to many abstract concepts specific dimensions of physical space — as when we
say we are feeling *down* or that things are looking *up*. When
something is unresolved or unknown, we also often associate it with being *up*. That's perhaps why we go to look
something *up* in the dictionary — because we aren't sure
what a word means. Or we say, "Why don't you *raise* that
question at the meeting?" Or "Bring that idea *up* on
Wednesday."

And when something is resolved we move in the oppo-
site direction. "Well, that *settles* it." Or "We finally got to the
bottom of this." Or "What it really comes *down* to is . . ."

And, again, although we use these words every day, we
aren't aware that we have almost no choice but to speak in
their terms.

And finally we might consider the spatial dimensions of a
word we use every day but seldom think of as spatial. I'm

thinking of the word "understand". What a strange word when looked at spatially. What kind of a relationship do we have with someone whom we "understand"?

So words themselves might be described as metaphors for nonverbal sense experience.

In this light, then, it is interesting to realize that the sensory data that arrive from the world around us are, and have been, the same for all humans everywhere. It is the interpretation of those data that has given us such widely differing views of reality — interpretations shaped by the metaphors of the particular language inside our minds to create the very different worlds outside.

It would almost seem as though we might posit a law of human perception: Sensory data do not become information until they have passed through mind and been filtered by language.

"Of shoes and ships and sealing wax . . ."

One of the unwritten laws that governs our thinking about almost everything might be put into words this way. Each language requires its speakers to break apart their experience of the world into bits and pieces that are in accord with the structural demands of that particular language.

Many people, I'm afraid, will find such a statement purely academic — that is, totally irrelevant to everyday concerns. I believe, however, that a moment's reflection may reveal that this statement about the influence of language on both our perception and thought may not be so irrelevant after all.

Let me express the idea again in the words of another writer, Benjamin Lee Whorf. In a short essay titled "Languages and Logic" written in 1941, Whorf said, "We cut up and arrange the spread and flow of events as we do largely because, through our mother tongue, we are parties to an agreement to do so, not because nature itself is segmented in exactly that way for all to see. Languages differ," he said, "not only in how they build their sentences but also in how they break down nature to secure the elements to put in those sentences."

In order for us to be able to communicate in English and its many related languages, we must first divide the continuum of sense experience into individual things — or nouns, as we call them. These literally form the subjects of our sentences and are the basis for our concept of what is, so to speak, "out there" — the shoes, the ships, the sealing wax, the cabbages and kings.

The next requirement for describing our experience is that these "things" must then do something or behave in some way. This second category of words we call verbs. So the world becomes rather arbitrarily and simplistically divided between "things" and what those "things" do. Certainly these divisions and classifications are not part of nature. They are created first in the human mind and then superimposed as a template on our experience. This template we call language.

And to make matters more complex, these "things", while treated structurally as all alike, are, in fact, often very different from each other. For example, "courage" as a noun has the same grammatical value and use as "chair" or "faucet". And yet it is clearly a concept of a totally different species. But it, along with words like "life" and "death", is treated grammatically as though it were interchangeable with "dog" and "ball".

So deeply rooted is the need to meet the grammatical

demands of our language for nouns that we will actually create them in our sentence structures when in fact there is serious doubt that any such "things" actually exist.

We look out the window, for instance, at the falling snow, and then we say, "*It* is snowing." But snowing is not a thing; it is a process. English structure, however, requires that we treat it as object. Thus we are forced to create an "it" as the subject of the verb "is", because to say "snowing" by itself is simply not enough — at least not in English.

Other languages whose origins are quite different from those of English might dissect experience in very unfamiliar but perfectly reasonable ways. Some Native American languages do just this. Instead of nouns we may find events or states of being that are classified according to their duration. Thus, for example, a sneeze, because it is of short duration, might be seen *only* as a verb — as a brief action. Yet a process expressed by the words "to educate" might be viewed as a noun because it is seen to have no meaning in the short term but only as measured over years or decades — its longevity making it a noun and, thus, providing for us a glimpse of the special value of time within that culture.

So it is possible to imagine a people whose language might dissect nature very differently than ours does — not into things and actions, but into processes that are of long or short duration, with a particular value given to stability over time. The result would be a world quite different from ours.

We often hear teachers advise the young to think clearly

in order to reach a solution to a problem. Sometimes this is an encouragement to think only in habitual patterns whose results are desirable because they are both familiar and predictable. The great revolutions in human thought, however, the ones that have shaped our history, have not come about so much by thinking clearly as by thinking differently.

The Evolution of Evolution

The name of Charles Darwin is, for most of us, synonymous with the word "evolution" — so much so that some people believe that evolution is something that Darwin himself discovered. But Darwin's great contribution was to define the process through which evolution expressed itself in nature. He called it natural selection.

Today we encounter the idea of evolution everywhere — in the book title on the evolution of economic theory, on the radio program on the evolution of rock music, or in a lecture about the evolution of jet aircraft.

Evolution is so much a part of the fabric of our thinking that it is hard for us to imagine that for centuries no such concept existed.

During the six or seven hundred years that followed the fall of the Roman empire, Western civilization found itself in the midst of what some historians have called the Dark Ages. Scholars of the time turned with envy and wonder toward the high culture and great learning that had flourished in ancient Greece and later in Rome but had now vanished in a turmoil of Barbarian invasions.

And the Church's view of human spiritual history seemed similarly downhill. For it was through disobedience, they said, that man and woman had been cast by God from the innocence and perfection of Eden's garden into a world of pain and suffering.

Thus, thoughtful people of the early Middle Ages looked longingly to the past as the source of everything that was desirable. In short, we might say that they saw their world as "devolutionary".

One exception to this sense of gloom and doom of the 12th and 13th centuries was found southwest of Paris in the town of Chartres. There, in association with the town's great cathedral, a school arose for the study of nature. Under the influence of two remarkable churchmen, a metaphorical bridge was built that linked the ancient Greek philosophers' fascination with order and harmony in nature to the pragmatic difficulties faced by the designers and builders of the great cathedrals of the Middle Ages.

In his excellent book *The Dawn of Modern Science*, Thomas Goldstein writes of the impact on medieval thought of the school at Chartres. The ideas of its leaders, he says, "all flow from this focusing . . . on nature as a vital, continuously creative force."

Based on this new view that nature was not simply the static creation of God, but a self-motivated creator and shaper of life in its own right, the school at Chartres began to perceive that the forces of nature could be systematically understood and put to use by the human mind. It was this idea that took Western thinking and its preoccupation with the past and turned it toward the possibilities of the future. The idea of evolution had been born.

Such changes in perception took decades and even centuries to infiltrate the existing devolutionary model of the world. And, as with all such changes, we see them reflected first in the way that the old meaning of words gave way to new.

Consider the word "improve". For us it means "to make better". But "improve" came into English in the 11th century with William the Conqueror from Normandy. It was made up of two French words "en" and "prouver", and for about 500 years it was a legal term used almost exclusively in business and in the English law courts. It meant only one thing: "to enclose and cultivate a piece of waste land for profit."

Then in the beginning of the 17th century, we find the word "improve" beginning to be used quite differently. It became a metaphor. The new meaning grew out of the sense that *if* somebody enclosed and cultivated a piece of waste land, they were making it better, more valuable, more productive. They were, as we would say, "improving" it.

In his fascinating book *History in English Words*, Owen Barfield reveals how in the 17th century the old meanings of other words were also changing. He speaks, for instance, of the word "progress" as coming to be used with something more like today's meaning with its sense of bettering the future. Prior to this, a "progress" had referred only to a journey made by a monarch around the kingdom. However, because some people were better off as a result of the monarch's visit — a new title to a brewer for a good bottle of ale or a military promotion for a good archer — the word "progress" became yet another metaphor for improvement.

Barfield's old friend C. S. Lewis writes of such shifts in perception in the epilogue to his book *The Discarded Image*. He says: "When changes in the human mind produce a sufficient disrelish of the old model and a sufficient hankering for a new one, phenomena to support the new one will obediently turn up."

Thus, Darwin's travels provided not only the natural phenomena but also the scientific basis to support this new model of the world that we describe today by the word "evolutionary".

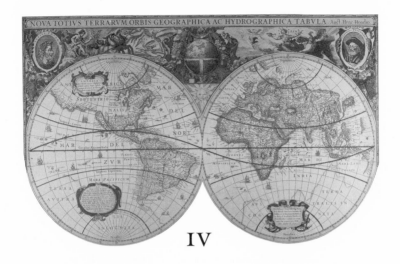

IV

The Dance of Mind with Nature

I believe it was Rudolph Steiner who said, "The mind is related to thought as the eye is to light." And so it is between those other two inseparable partners, mind and nature.

The Taj Mahal

Many of you have probably seen pictures of this remarkable structure with its huge marble dome rising from the roof like a white pearl above four smaller cupolas, and the whole structure guarded by four marble minarets that stand at each corner of the square base on which the building rests. Some fewer of you, perhaps, may actually have been there, and you will be familiar with it in a different way.

Some people think of it as a king's palace or as a mosque for Islamic worshipers. But the Taj Mahal is a tomb. It was built by the great Mughal Emperor of India, Shah Jahan, in memory of his wife, Mumtaz Mahal, who died at the age of thirty-nine shortly after giving birth to their fourteenth child. That was in 1631.

The following year, while still in mourning, Shah Jahan began work on what he wanted to be the most beautiful memorial ever built. It was to be situated in northern India at the Mughal capital of Agra on the south bank of the Jumana river. The Taj, itself, took twelve years to complete, but its elaborate gate, beautiful gardens, and several outbuildings were not finished until 1654, twenty-two years after the work had first begun. After his own death, Shah Jahan was buried in the Taj Mahal next to his wife.

History records that there were 20,000 workmen employed in the project: carpenters, stone masons, blacksmiths, calligraphers, goldsmiths, and gem cutters. One thousand elephants were used to bring the white marble from the Makarana quarries in Rajastan 120 miles away. Some carried pieces weighing more than two tons, while even larger blocks were pulled in huge wooden wagons by teams of twenty or thirty water buffalo. Precious and semi-precious stones to be inlaid in the marble in intricate patterns of vines and petaled flowers were brought from everywhere in the East: turquoise from Tibet, jade and crystal from China, carnelian from Baghdad, lapis lazuli from Afghanistan, and from the Himalayan mountains of Nepal came agate, black marble, and amethyst. In all, some forty-three different kinds of gemstones were used. Thus, a single inlaid flower blossom only an inch across may contain as many as thirty or forty separate pieces of stone, and the blossoms, vines, and leaves are everywhere — on the ceilings, on the walls and on the tombs — a perpetual garden in stone.

On average, there are each day between four and five thousand visitors to the Taj. It has been viewed and painted and photographed and written about by literally millions of people over 350 years.

In January of 1995, on a foggy rain-washed morning before dawn, I visited the Taj Mahal. I was there as part of a team of Americans who were discussing with Indian authorities ways to improve the economic conditions of local people by developing the international tourist potential of the Taj and the other great Mughal monuments in and around Agra City.

Three of us had gone that morning hoping to see the Taj at sunrise, but as we walked the long path through the formal gardens, the dense fog made the Taj itself invisible. Because of the weather and the hour, there was no one there. We walked silently by the side of the long reflecting pool. As we approached the end of the garden, the huge dome loomed out of the white mist and seemed to float in the air above us.

A guard was there to meet us. He took us into the tomb room and there opened a padlock on a side door. Behind it was a network of empty rooms and a steep marble stairway leading to the roof. Coming out of the dim light of the stairs onto the roof into the swirling fog, we found ourselves at the foot of the great circular drum of marble some forty feet high that is the base for the towering pearl-white dome. Its top vanished into the mist — white dissolving into white.

We talked for a while in hushed tones. Then, more out of curiosity than anything else, I asked our guide if there were a way to see the inside of the dome itself. He smiled and said nothing. But fumbling in an inside pocket of his over-coat he soon produced another key and, holding it up, he beckoned with it for me to follow him. My two colleagues were deep in discussion over some aspect of Mughal architecture and waved to me to go alone. So it was only I who followed the guide around to the opposite side of the great marble drum to where there was a small louvered door. He bent and worked at the padlock that had apparently not been opened for a long time. The door was stuck. And as he strained to pull outward, it suddenly burst open.

There was a rush of sound like the blowing of a strong wind. And then the stench of manure. Inside I saw a steep marble staircase leading up into darkness. The steps were alive with bats. They slithered and flopped under our feet; they landed on our heads and shoulders, their high shrieking in our ears. With wings ten to twelve inches across, they seemed huge. I saw the guide dig furiously at one that had disappeared into the woolen scarf around his neck. He was obviously afraid of being bitten. Thoughts of rabies and India's recent outbreak of plague raced through my mind. But the guide had started up the stairs. Bats swooped down and past us, fleeing through the open door. We stopped at the top of the stairs. It was very hot and the smell overpowering. I didn't want to breathe in the fetid air. We were in a darkness quite unlike anything I had ever experienced before. It was an ancient and permanent darkness, made by man, not like that of night. No new dawn ever drove these shadows back. There had been no sunlight here for 350 years.

My guide turned on his small flashlight. Above us, the black air was alive with bats that fluttered like dead leaves rising and falling on a wind. Beyond them in the weak light of the torch, at the very edge of this dark universe, I could just see the inner curve of the huge dome as it disappeared above me into blackness, much as the white dome outside had vanished in the mist. I turned and led the way back down the narrow stairs and emerged with relief into the fog and a semblance of daylight.

Although I had visited the Taj many years before, this experience changed the way I have come to see it. For I am aware now of a polarity in its nature that I had not seen before. It is the polarity not only between light and dark but also between the façade of physical beauty and great art that stands in harsh contrast to the long centuries of violent and brutal Mughal rule in India.

Most commonly, we think of polarity as applying to electricity or magnetism in ways that we describe using words like "positive" and "negative", or "attraction" and "repulsion". But as we look deeper, we see that our entire relation to nature is shaped by this concept of polarity. Something that is "up" can only be understood in the context of something that is "down". Every "front" creates a "back". Every "beginning" leads to an "ending". In this context, the relationship between "subject" and "object" or between "inside" and "outside" takes on an entirely new meaning. While we are able to perceive each pole as distinct from the other, we also realize that they are impossible to separate. Now consider the statement "every rose has its thorns". Is it a statement only about those particuar things, or does it lead us into a very different world in which roses and thorns "mean" something else? And how then do we separate roses and thorns as objects from roses and thorns as meaning?

When we ask what something means, we do not find the answer only outside us. Meaning grows from the way in which the mind itself dances with nature. Whatever is outside us is defined by what is inside. And the tension between them is the dynamic of the dance.

The British writer Owen Barfield once said, "I have reached the conclusion that the natural world can only be understood in depth as a series of images symbolizing concepts."

Thus the Taj Mahal has come to mean something quite different for me than it once did.

Thou and It

The name of Henri Frankfort is not exactly a household word. Nor is the title of the book that he co-authored in the early 1940s called *The Intellectual Adventure of Ancient Man*. Frankfort was from Holland, and in the 1920s he became director of the Egypt exploration society in London. Later, at the University of Chicago, he directed archeological studies in Iraq for the famous Oriental Institute.

Frankfort was particularly interested in how early people saw their world in comparison to how we in Western cultures today see ours. He didn't fall prey to the assumption that the words "early" or "primitive" are synonyms for backward and ignorant.

Frankfort wrote:

> The fundamental difference between the attitudes of modern and ancient man as regards the surrounding world is this: for modern, scientific man, the phenomenal world is primarily an "it"; for ancient — and for primitive man — it is a "thou". This does not mean that primitive man, in order to explain natural phenomena, imparts human characteristics

to an inanimate world. Primitive man simply does not know an inanimate world. Every phenomenon which confronts him — the thunderclap, the sudden shadow, the eerie and unknown clearing in the wood — the stone that hurts him while on a hunting trip — any phenomenon may face him at any time not as "it" but as "thou".

The vast difference between the view of nature as "thou" and as "it" reveals something of the way that the human mind itself has evolved. It speaks not so much of growing intelligence in humans over time but of a substantive change in the way that humans have come to perceive their world.

In its earliest stages, human consciousness as revealed in the ritual and art of so-called primitive peoples perceived nature and "being" as inseparable. There was no self-awareness of the kind that we take for granted today, and what we now call the psyche was seen by early humans to be reflected in the phenomena of nature. Then gradually over time, and I would suggest paralleling the development of language, "thou" or "being" became separated from nature and internalized in us as the human psyche or self-consciousness — that sense of "me". It was through this process that nature became an "it" and today has come to appear to us as a collection of physical objects ranging from atoms to galaxies that are exclusively physical, chemical, and biological, and governed by what we describe as the "laws of nature". And so complete today is this apparent separation of the "me" from the "it" that the laws of nature themselves are seen purely as properties of an external physical world rather than as metaphors created by the human mind.

Thus the evolution of human perception from experiencing nature as "thou" to the objective exploitation of nature as "it" has led us into a world that we are able to manipulate with increasing and even frightening skill, but which is also, for many, increasingly devoid of meaning. It seems to me that the environmental movement of recent decades, at least in part and wearing many different guises, represents an unconscious effort to reestablish "being" in nature. Whether it be saving the whales, or creating rights for animals, or protecting the northern spotted owl, these seem to me an indication of a need, at least for some, for a psychic "other" than ourselves and the need to recreate a nature whose "being" is in some way an extension of our own.

In a sense, all of us have been through this process before in that early discovery of our bodies as part of our own being. Joseph Church in his interesting book *Language and the Discovery of Reality* describes this process. Speaking of the very young child, he says:

> When shortly before six months, he discovers his hands explicitly and visually, it is as external objects. More striking still, is the baby's discovery of his or her feet, which he treats as alien entities — and which his now active hands capture and bring to his mouth for tasting. When he bites on his toes, he seems surprised that it hurts.

Doesn't this sound surprisingly like our recent growing

awareness that nature may in fact be an extension of us — that when we "bite" her, as it were, it is we who are hurt? To understand that those external objects that we call nature may be an extension of our own being, much as our bodies are, is an unfamiliar perspective for us. It requires a redefining of the meaning of self that transcends both individual mind and body.

Is it possible, then, that our present capacity for self-awareness, so recently developed and yet assumed to be so permanent, is but a stage in the evolution of human consciousness on its way to an entirely new understanding of the meaning of being? Humankind, in the process of coming to observe nature as object, created the only environment from which the observer could also become aware of the self as distinguishable from nature. And thus the separation of "thou" from "it" was complete. Clearly the next step in this evolution would seem to lie in our conscious recognition that, although we can distinguish between the outer and the inner worlds, their apparent separation is, in fact, an illusion. Isn't this the real meaning of "at-one-ment"?

Indoors — Outdoors

Some years ago there was a popular cartoonist by the name of Walt Kelly. Readers may recall his character Pogo, a small, furry, 'possum-like figure from the Okefenokee Swamp, who shared with his friends Albert the alligator and a turtle named Churchy la Femme a variety of adventures that mirrored the human condition in America during some difficult times in the '50s and '60s.

Like many humorists and satirists, Walt Kelly was a serious and thoughtful person. Before he became well known, I recall hearing him give a talk on the freshness of perception of the very young. He felt that little children had not yet learned to project already predetermined meanings onto their experiences, as we adults tend to do. By way of illustration, he described how one day his young son had come up to him and asked, "Daddy, why is it that people always build their houses outdoors?"

It is a lovely question, and it has many implications.

In our culture, that doorway represents a kind of illusory

dividing line. Inside is our world; outside is what we have learned to call nature. So ingrained is this dividing line created by the doorway that we refer to someone who likes to climb mountains and hunt, to canoe and fish, as an "outdoorsman". We even have magazines called *Outdoors* and *Outdoor Life*. Thus, for us, that doorway has become an important frame of reference, but for the most part an unconscious one.

I tell the story of Walt Kelly's son and his delightful question because in that strange dualism of "outdoors" and "indoors" we have the opportunity to see clearly two elements, each of which provides the environment from which the other may be seen. In fact, oddly enough, neither one can exist without the other. If you attempt to remove one part, the other disappears as well.

A similar relationship exists between other pairs of concepts like "front" and "back" or "up" and "down". And is it possible that the idea of something being "infinite" really has no meaning except as it starts at a particular point in space and time called the "finite"? Could a similar relation be said to exist between "consciousness" and "unconsciousness", or between "maleness" and "femaleness"?

My point might be better expressed as a corollary applicable to all perception: it is impossible to perceive any environment except from the context of another one. We can find any number of proverbs that illustrate this. "You never miss the water 'til the well runs dry," or "only the blind know what it really means to see."

In a slightly different way, we see this corollary at work when we hear of the Peace Corps volunteer from Akron, Ohio, who has spent two years in Kenya. She can never return to Akron and see it as she did before she left. She has an entirely different environment of experience from which to measure everything American.

So this corollary functions across time as well as space. Wasn't this what St. Paul was expressing when he wrote in his first letter to the Corinthians, "When I was a child I spake as a child, I understood as a child, I thought as a child"? Certainly this isn't a statement that a child would make. It is only meaningful from another perspective in time.

Different historic periods, then, represent different environments of thought from which people may become aware of different ways of looking at the world at other times. Youth or old age might be considered such environments, but so too are the Middle Ages or the Renaissance. Neither of those familiar labels was applied historically much before the 17th or 18th centuries.

So we might say that it is only from a different environment in time that any era can be encompassed by the mind and even given a name.

It makes one wonder how our own time will be described by future historians. If they were to label us, say, as the "objectivists", as the people who believed that objects could exist independently of subjects, we might feel surprised, perhaps, and even a bit defensive. For their description of us would suggest that our way of seeing is only a subjective perspective — not unlike the way we look upon the "superstitious" beliefs of the Middle Ages. We are convinced that our view of the world is based on the hard facts of both sense experience and objective analysis. So we might say to them, "Of course we believe in the nuts and bolts reality of the physical world. After all that's just common sense."

The question is whether 500 years from now that "sense" will still be commonly shared, or will people by then have come to understand that the objective world and the subjective world have no meaning except in terms of each other — a relationship that seems very similar indeed to the one we discovered earlier between "indoors" and "outdoors".

The Inside of Nature

Some years ago, I was invited by the Peace Corps to go to Honduras. They had asked me to consider ways that Peace Corps volunteers there might be helpful in increasing the awareness of local people about critical environmental issues.

In almost every developing country today, one finds a vast information base on the environment ranging over such topics as soil types, forest cover, wildlife populations, and land use. Our international assistance agencies have done a lot of homework, and while such information is vital to understanding local environmental problems, it describes only what I would call the "outside" of nature.

There is an entirely different dimension of nature that very few environmentalists are concerned with at all. And I would call this the "inside" of nature. It includes the shaping force of language, history, and culture on the way that local people perceive their natural surroundings. These ways of looking are far more difficult to quantify than water resources and soil types, but they affect absolutely everything. The problem is that they operate in ways of which the local people and the environmentalist are often entirely unconscious. They, in fact, help to define the different meanings of the word "environment" in different cultures.

The European domination of Honduras began in 1524 with the arrival of Hernando Cortés, fresh from his victory over the Aztec empire in Mexico. He and his men brought with them the Spanish language and the Roman Catholic religion. Cortés had come from Spain, a country that in 1492 had defeated the last stronghold of the Arabic Moors at the city of Grenada — thus ending nearly 750 years of Arab domination in Spain. One cannot help but wonder about the unconscious layers of centuries of Arabic influence coupled with Spanish values and attitudes that Cortés and his men brought to Honduras.

The Spanish language itself tends to polarize the world into objects that are either masculine or feminine — indicated by the articles "el" or "la". The sun is masculine — "el sol". The earth is feminine — "la tierra". And nature herself is — "la naturaleza".

The Spanish concept of masculinity, expressed so popularly in the words "macho" and "machismo" is redolent with many implied but unstated attitudes toward what is female. In this same context, one wonders about the influence on the Spanish of Arabic attitudes toward the female as someone who must always be under the constraint and control of men — for her own benefit and for protection from her own irrational and emotional nature. Is it also possible that nature as woman is to be dominated and used for the benefit of man in a similar way?

One day I raised this question, but only half seriously, with a group of Spanish language trainers employed by the Peace Corps, all of whom were Hondurans. "Let us say," I suggested, by way of illustrating a point about the Spanish language, "that many of the environmental problems in Honduras are a reflection of male attitudes toward woman. We would have to describe this in Spanish as 'el problema' — the problem — as masculine. And if we wished to encourage a more caring attitude toward the environment, we would have to call this in Spanish 'la soluccion' — the solution — as feminine. So 'el problema,'" I continued, "could be said to represent the entire history of Honduras in terms of what has happened to its natural environment, and 'la soluccion' would represent its future, if it is going to have any."

My experience in Central America had suggested that there are at least two very different concepts of woman. There is the woman to be exploited as in nature — "la naturaleza" — but there is also woman as sacrosanct as in mother — "la madre". La madre as the origin of life and as chief nourisher and protector of the family transcends the idea of exploitation and in a Catholic country is closely associated with the Virgin Mary. "Why not, then," I suggested, "begin to introduce the local people to the idea of nature not as 'la naturaleza' but as 'la madre'?"

The language teachers were silent. Then one of them, a woman, spoke. "I don't believe any of us have talked of these things very much," she said. "And it is true that in our country the exploitation of the environment often comes from powerful men — from the politicians, the generals, and the businessmen. It is they who control the land and the resources. Certainly they represent 'el problema'. But what can anyone do?"

I thought about her question. "Perhaps," I said, "it might be possible, instead of confronting the men directly, to educate their wives about environmental issues through your various women's groups and then let them confront their husbands at home."

She smiled. "That would truly be," she said, "'la soluccion.'"

Mind over Matter

I used to ask my students at the University of Vermont to list the resources that would be crucial to our future survival as a species. As most of us would, they responded by naming things such as water, soil, clean air, or oil. If they were questioned as to why they didn't include such important resources as courage, commitment, or honesty, they would say that these were not "natural" resources. Even if they could understand that honesty might possibly be as crucial a part of environmental quality as clean air, they still remained skeptical about its being a natural resource. For them, as for most of us, the environment, along with all of nature and its resources, is "outside, over there", separate from us.

So deeply ingrained is this habit of our thinking that it has become an unexamined belief — one that unconsciously shapes our entire perception of what we call nature. And when we discover that we share that habit of thinking in common with many other people in our culture, we describe it simply as "common sense". And for us that's the way the world really is. The underlying premises remain unquestioned because we aren't conscious of them.

Let's look at another habit of thinking.

Imagine we were to take a walk in the woods. We might find ourselves crossing a narrow stream, and there we notice that ten or twelve small stones have been removed from the stream and laid by the side of the path in the shape of an arrow. Clearly someone has done this, and so we feel no hesitation in arguing that the arrow of stones is a manifestation of mind. It is not the individual stones themselves that reveal the presence of mind. We would say it was their pattern. But then if we looked to either side of the stone arrow, we might see a tree. We would be able to identify it, too, by its pattern of bark, its leaf shape, and even its overall outline. But it would never occur to us to suggest that its pattern was a manifestation of mind. We would say it was an object.

For us, mind is assumed to be something contained in our heads. And while we would perhaps agree that our heads and our bodies are objects like the tree, we would insist there is something more inside us that is not just object. So strong is this conviction that we resent it when hospitals, airlines, and governments treat us as if we were only objects. We insist that we be treated as people — that unique combination of object and mind. But it never occurs to us to attribute this same dual nature to nature herself. For us nature is only object, whether the nature to which we refer is maple tree, atom, or galaxy.

There are two unquestioned assumptions on which we base this belief. The first is that mind, our mind, evolved over millions of years out of mindless matter. And the second assumption is that mind is limited to humans and a few of the higher animals.

All around us everyday we see countless objects that are manifestations of mind: computers, screwdrivers, books, houses, cars, television sets, and scud missiles. And while our senses perceive them as separate and distinct from us, we can perhaps understand, when we stop to think about it, that they came into existence only through mind — our mind. But we find it almost impossible to entertain the idea that the maple tree by the path, or the frog in the stream, or even we ourselves are products of mind. These, we say, are the result of mindless evolution, shaped by a randomly operating process called natural selection. And when we say this we forget that the concept of evolution itself is a product of mind — a way of thinking that must precede our capacity to see nature in that particular way. And to further confound our certainty about what is object and what is mind — of what is outside us and what is inside — today we are told by the particle physicists that the ultimate constituents of all matter appear not as objects but as energy fields — states of being which, in some instances we are told, have no mass and cannot be said even to occupy space.

I am reminded of a comment made earlier this century

by Sir James Jeans, the respected physicist, astronomer, and mathematician. "Today," he said, "there is wide agreement . . . that the stream of knowledge is heading toward a non-mechanical reality; the universe," he concluded, "begins to look more like a great thought than like a great machine."

Perhaps we could say this is just another illustration of the power of "mind over matter".

". . . to talk of many things."

In February of 1992, I went to Caracas, Venezuela, as one of 1,500 international delegates attending the Fourth World Congress on National Parks and Protected Areas.

The history of this meeting dates back to the summer of 1962 when representatives of the world's national parks and protected areas first gathered at the Seattle World's Fair. Every decade since then, a different nation has hosted the meeting. In 1992, Venezuela hosted the largest conference of its kind that had ever been held. Its purpose was to discuss the myriad problems faced by the world's natural areas — problems that are not unlike those faced by the planet earth itself: resource depletion, population pressures, dwindling economic reserves, and political upheaval.

Because I had been invited to present a paper at the opening session of the conference, I was naturally curious when I received in the mail a listing of the titles of the many other papers that were to be given during the ten days of meetings. Included were such topics as:

"Democracy, Protected Areas and the Politician's Perspective"

"How Debt, Trade, Exchange Rates, Inflation, and Macroeconomics Affect Biological Diversity"

"Developing an Investment Portfolio for Supporting Natural Areas"

"Giving Evolution a Helping Hand by Restoring Ecosystems"

"Building Protected Areas to Withstand Civil Strife"

And, finally, my favorite title listed under a workshop on coastal zone management — a talk called "Kinorhynches, Echiurans, Priapulans, and Sipunculans — How to Manage Them When You Can't Even Pronounce Them".

Well, those were only a fraction of the topics, but almost all of them are focused on techniques of management, on the importance of scientific research, and on economic and political considerations. Certainly no one can question the validity of such concerns, but their primary emphasis seems to be on nature as utility, and I find that leaves something missing.

Suppose we were to compare one of the world's great national parks to a giant building — one that we did not create ourselves, perhaps, but which we believe in some way is important to preserve. And let us say that a conference had been convened modeled on the one in Venezuela, devoted to the preservation of that building. Such a conference, then, would be concerned almost exclusively with what I would call our custodial relation to the structure. Through science, we have ways to measure with extreme precision the height, the length, and the volume of the entire building. We note that part of the roof is leaking, or that some of the beautiful and ancient stained glass windows need releading. We need more chairs for the increasing number of visitors. The entrance needs painting, and, inside, the collection of rare artifacts is in need of maintenance. This is our role as scientific "janitors".

But suppose that one day it was discovered that the great building is, in fact, a part of a huge university. Then, and only then, would we realize that our concern had been with the fact of the structure and not its meaning or purpose — that up until then no one had asked what the building was for.

If it were part of a great university, would it not be appropriate to have on its staff professors of literature, art, and philosophy as well as highly trained janitors?

Surely it is important to catalog the books belonging to the university, to assess their condition periodically, and to arrange them in some accessible order, and, yes, even to call attention to their diversity. But is it not equally important to ask what the books mean? If this is so, then to whom would you address your questions — to the custodial staff or to the professors of literature, art, and philosophy?

It is because of our unquestioned assumption that our only relation to nature is physical that we hold conferences about nature focused primarily on concerns that are economic or scientific.

Owen Barfield gives expression to these ideas in his small book of essays *The Rediscovery of Meaning*. "It remains to be considered," he says, "whether the future development of scientific man must inevitably continue in the same direction, so that he becomes more and more a mere onlooker, measuring with greater and greater precision and manipulating more and more cleverly an earth to which he grows spiritually more and more a stranger. His detachment has enabled him to describe, weigh, and measure the processes of nature and to a large extent to control them; but the price he has paid has been the loss of his grasp of any meaning in either nature or himself."

Hail Columbia

I am indebted to my British friend Rupert Sheldrake —
scientist, author, and philosopher — for the discussions
that led to many of the ideas expressed in this essay.

If you were to ask a cross-section of the American public
who Christopher Columbus was, you'd probably get a
pretty well informed response. But if you asked instead,
"Who was Columbia?", their confusion would be almost
complete. Perhaps if reminded that some of the best wind
surfing in America occurs at a place called the Columbia
River Gorge, or that our nation's capitol is located in the
District of Columbia, they would probably acknowledge
that the name Columbia is familiar and would point out
the existence of a prominent university by that name, as
well as a movie studio on the West Coast and a radio and
television corporation on the East. But most people will
know almost nothing about who Columbia was.

The word Columbia and the word America share something in common in that they are the feminization of the
names of men. But they are something else as well — some-

thing that is perhaps best revealed by the two songs "America the Beautiful", with which we are all familiar, and the other, which most of us have forgotten or never knew, "Columbia, the Gem of the Ocean". On closer inspection we find that the words are female metaphors for the lands presumably discovered by Amerigo Vespucci and Christopher Columbus.

It requires only a short journey into the shadowy but illuminating world of metaphor to find this "female" continent in its early days described as "virgin" territory. A bit later, history texts speak of intrepid male explorers "penetrating the wilderness", and still later they tell of that particular chapter of the American saga that is always referred to as the "opening up of the West". It would be hard to imagine language more sexist in tone and implication. So perhaps the important question is not "Who *was* Columbia?", but "What became of her?"

In a way, the feminine spirit of America has gone underground. Certainly our international persona is more characteristically represented by the male figure of Uncle Sam wearing the stars and stripes, and the words "Yank" and "Yankee" are almost synonymous for male and military. So looking at us from the outside, it is hard to see anything of the female spirit of this country. It is almost as though we feared to reveal that important side of our being as a nation.

Perhaps some Americans see the Statue of Liberty as the personification of the feminine spirit of our country. Maybe it is she who has taken on Columbia's role. But even she has a gender problem. We might have been reminded of this, had we been aware of such things, at the time of the protests by Chinese students in Tienamen Square.

As part of their protest, they had erected the figure of a woman whom they named the "Goddess of Democracy" or the "Goddess of Freedom". Interestingly, she was always referred to by them as a "Goddess". Our symbol for liberty, on the other hand, is almost always referred to as the "Statue of Liberty". The word "statue", however, has no gender. Thus, quite unconsciously, we seem to have neutered her.

So where do we search for the lost spirit of this land — the one we once called Columbia? I would suggest that we find her to begin with in our great national parks. One might even say that the National Park Service has been entrusted with the stewardship of those particularly unusual embodiments of Columbia that we have labeled Yellowstone, Grand Teton, Yosemite, or Glacier. In this sense, these areas are symbols of spirit as much as they are physical attractions or entertainment for tourists. They are manifestations of her being — not simply collections of natural phenomena. If we understand even dimly that this is so, what better effort for the National Park Service to perform than, while others each year celebrate the masculine initiative of Columbus, to attempt to resurrect the faded memory of the lost Columbia — to promote the rebirth of her spirit in the land and to allow her to come to consciousness — first within the parks, which are her shrines, and then throughout the land?

The difficulty is that to accomplish this would require a very different way of looking at our parks, our nation, and ourselves.

The Early Exploration of Space

Recently I was looking at a collection of old magazine covers drawn by Norman Rockwell. I found myself thinking about the value that we in the West place on an artist's ability to represent three-dimensional space on a two-dimensional surface. The popularity of Norman Rockwell's drawings seems to confirm the appeal of that technique. Although many people may find his subject matter appealing, I rather think the main attraction lies in his ability to depict the world as we might say, "so realistically". It was thoughts like these that reminded me of that revolution in our perception of the world that began in the 14th century.

The earliest concern in western Europe with representing three-dimensional space seems to have begun in the early 1300s with the work of Italian artists like Giotto. The historian Thomas Goldstein in his book *The Dawn of Modern Science* writes of these early efforts. "Oddly, the method used to convey this illusion [of space]," he says, "was not the application of the laws of perspective. . . . Rather it was a conceptual development, the reflection of a new attitude of mind."

This new interest in the representation of space apparently went hand in hand with the rediscovery of nature and that growing fascination with the material world of the senses that was the signature of the Renaissance.

Throughout much of the Middle Ages prior to that time, artistic representations had been concerned with the timeless and the spiritual, not with flesh and blood or the here and now. Since the subject matter of most painting had been primarily religious, it was viewed as much with the mind's eye as with the physical eye, the figures seeming to float in a space that was both eternal and dimensionless.

In 1435, more than a century after Giotto's death, the Italian humanist and architect Leon Battista Alberti published a book titled *On Painting*. In it he described the laws for creating linear perspective based on the principle that on a flat surface all parallel lines must converge at a point. It was a device that enabled the artist to locate his subject in "real" space as seen through the eyes of a particular viewer who is, in this sense, always you.

Eight years earlier, the young Italian painter Masaccio, using this technique, had created on the wall of a church in Florence the mural of an adjoining chapel that was so lifelike that, as one historian writes, "For an instant the viewers thought they were looking at the real thing."

In the hands of these artists, space became as tangible a part of sense experience as the very objects that defined it. The new illusion of depth was part of a changing vision of everything. It was part of the exciting discovery and experience of the earth's own curvature into three dimensions — a knowledge of which was crucial to the great voyages of discovery and to the making of accurate maps.

Indeed, Alberti, himself, in writing about the laws of perspective, was apparently influenced by the difficulties of early mapmakers in representing the curvature of the earth on a flat surface. The grid provided by the intersecting lines of latitude and longitude became a model for superimposing a similar grid on all of nature to assist the artist in reproducing it in three dimensions — much like seeing the world through a mullioned window.

So it seems more than just coincidence that the year 1453, when Nicholas Copernicus first published his hypothesis that the sun and not the earth was the center of the universe, was the same year that Andreas Vesalius published his book on human anatomy. The unknown artist of Vesalius' book provided a macabre view of the bones, the muscles, and the organs of multiple human bodies drawn in three dimensions against the backdrop of the Italian countryside.

It was a such a view of reality as the world had never seen — a view made possible only through the artist's eye and skill.

Vesalius had turned the human body inside out, while Copernicus had done the same to the heavens. Inner space and outer space and all their contents were on their way to becoming objectified. And in the far distance beyond the curve of the horizon of time, one might have seen the approach of the scientific revolution. Galileo, Tycho Brahe, Kepler, and, later, Descartes and Newton, would each take his turn in the exploration of space. And the world would never again be the same.

The Spirit in the Stone

My first visit to the Louvre took place on a bright mid-summer day, more years ago than I care to remember. My recollection is that a major renovation of the building was underway and several of the galleries were closed to the public. Perhaps it was this that explained why, in my memory, so few people were there.

It now seems a strange experience to have wandered about alone that day with neither knowledge nor purpose, among some of the greatest works of art in the world. To say that I approached the experience of the Louvre with an open mind would not be quite accurate. Better perhaps to describe it as an empty mind totally unaware of its own emptiness. During the course of that visit I encountered for my first time the Venus de Milo, the Mona Lisa, and works by Botticelli, Raphael, and Rembrandt. My sense was of being in the presence of the great and the famous without understanding their greatness and being only vaguely aware of their fame.

It was in the very entrance hall of the Louvre that I had

an experience that might be described as one that brought me to my senses. To the left of the hall was a wide staircase that led to the second floor. On the landing of that staircase, where it divided right and left, stood the ancient statue known to the Greeks as Nike and to us as the Winged Victory of Samothrace.

As I approached the stairs, the sculpture soared above me — a massive, and now headless, female figure with huge outstretched wings — the fluid movement of the body clearly revealed through the marble robes, the right leg bent in striving forward, the left leg back. It seemed alive, in the very act of launching itself into flight over my head.

I was completely unprepared for the impact of that sculpture. It inspired in me a sense of involuntary awe with which I was unfamiliar. Climbing the stairway, I was forced to look upward to see it — forced to assume a physical posture that one could only associate with reverence. Reaching the landing where it stood, I felt dwarfed by its size and power — qualities that were strangely enhanced by the absolute stillness of the empty museum. A plaque at the base of the sculpture briefly described its history. I remember only that it said it was made of Parian marble.

I thought long about that sculpture of victory written in stone. Why, I asked myself, would someone choose to express the idea of flight in marble? Flight is transcendent. It is not of the earth. It is of the air. Stone is the very opposite — weighed down by the burden of its own gravity, seeking earth. I could almost imagine an artist working in chicken wire and papier mâché — something light and malleable, something more like flight itself — even perhaps using real feathers on the wings and real cloth in which to drape the great female body.

As I thought of the artist working in marble, hammer and chisel chipping away the stone flakes to reveal that remarkable image hidden in the stone, I realized then that marble was the perfect medium to express the freedom of flight. At some point, sensed only by the artist himself, the heaviness of stone and the lightness of flight would create such tension, the one in the other, that the body and wings would finally break forth from their stone prison and soar into space. It was through this conflict between the properties of stone and the idea of flight that the artist made his statement — a statement in which he expressed what was inside himself only through shaping what was outside.

But there was something else that made me thoughtful — something whose implications reached far beyond this remarkable sculpture.

It is our unquestioned belief today that over millions of years a force in nature that we call evolution was responsible for the development of organic life out of inorganic molecular matter. This in turn led to the earliest single-celled organisms, and thus began the long process that produced through the random action of natural selection the vast diversity of living organisms including humans and the human mind. The assumption that lies behind such a history is that mind evolved by accident from mindless matter.

One wonders what would happen if an alien race from another planet were to encounter the Winged Victory of Samothrace as the only manifestation of the human mind on earth. Would they deduce that the origin of the mind that produced the sculpture could be found by studying the history of the marble? Or would they perhaps conclude, as the sculpture itself suggests, that mind is something of an altogether different nature than the matter through which it manifests itself?

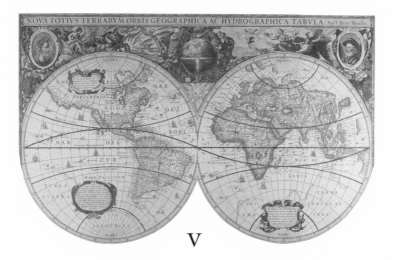

V

Thought and Things

Our world is deluged by data and facts. Our culture awards prizes to those people who store up the greatest amount of information in memory, even when they may not understand the meaning of what they know.

The following essays suggest a distinction between what something is and what something means — between knowing and understanding.

The Diversity of Life

I recently finished reading biologist E. O. Wilson's remarkable book *The Diversity of Life*. I came away not only with a sense of wonder at the staggering complexity of the intricate biological dance between genes and their environment, but also with the heightened pleasure that comes from simply being in the presence of a first-rate mind.

It is a mind immersed in the world of fact.

Wilson states that he recently estimated the number of known species of living organisms to be 1.4 million. This includes all plants, animals, and micro-organisms that have been identified to date. And then to illustrate how little, in fact, we know about life, he adds that this estimate may be less than 1/10th of the total number of species that actually live on earth. He describes research that has counted between 4,000 and 5,000 different species of bacteria in a single gram of forest soil in Norway. From one single tree in a forest in southeast Peru he identified forty-three species of ants in twenty-six genera — a number, he says, equal to "the entire ant fauna of the British Isles." He details the episodic catastrophes throughout geologic history that have led to the die-off of countless species, and he describes the capacity of the survivors to diversify by natural selection to fill every environmental niche with new forms of life. And finally he provides us with a litany of place names covering virtually the entire planet where species of all kinds are threatened today by human activity.

Conservatively, he estimates the loss of species at 27,000 a year, seventy-two every day, and three each hour.

I come away from the mass of data and the years of research, and I am moved by the learning and the labor of love represented by this excellent book. But it also makes me thoughtful about something else — and that is the difference between what things are and what things mean. Let me explain.

目 玉 焼

If I were to show you a series of three Japanese characters that form a single word, you could learn that the first character, a vertical rectangle divided evenly into thirds by two horizontal lines, originated as a representation of the human eye. You might also learn that in Japanese when this figure accompanies other characters to form a single word, it is pronounced "may".

The second figure is a symbolic representation of the role of the emperor in providing order for the universe. The emperor is depicted as a vertical line that passes through and connects three evenly spaced horizontal lines one above the other. The uppermost line represents the heavens, the middle line humanity, and the bottom line the earth. So the ruler is one who binds his subjects in unity with the cosmos in which they live. But in this particular character, there is also a small slash downward from left to right across its lower right-hand corner. Our study might reveal that originally this slash was drawn as a small circle to represent the emperor's material wealth as symbolized by the shape of a pearl. Later on, for ease of drawing, the circle evolved into a slash. The idea of the pearl, however, still lingers even today, as the whole figure has come to represent "roundness" as in the shape of a ball. It is pronounced "dama".

The third character, the most complex, consists of three small plus marks that are placed above what seems to be a table or bench. To their left is what might be a stylized representation of the flames of a fire. The plus marks are a symbol for flowers growing from earth. So the picture is of soil on a table being burned by fire. It represents a kiln in the process of firing clay pottery and is used as a metaphor for anything cooked or burnt. It is pronounced "yake".

So we have three elaborate figures, each with its own history of evolving shape and form. Together they are pronounced "may-dama-yake".

With training, and in time, we might become expert in understanding the evolution of all such forms in the Japanese language. We could, as well, learn to count and measure with great precision the number of component strokes of which each figure is constituted. We might study the long history that dictates the specific order in which those lines are to be applied to paper with brush and ink. Next we might attempt to record the thousands of such characters of the Japanese language in a single book, carefully weighing each page before and after the character is drawn. The difference in weight between the blank page and the printed page would tell us the amount of ink that constitutes the entire language. We could do all of this and more, but none of our activity would tell us what the language means.

Loosely translated, "may-dama-yake" means "burned eyeball". It is a word one would use in a Japanese restaurant to order a fried egg "sunny side up". For me it is a lovely illustration of the difference between what something is and what something means.

Topsy Turvy

For the next few minutes I would like to write about some things about which I know practically nothing.

I am a subscriber to *Discover* magazine, which, as its masthead announces, is concerned with "the world of science". Whether we like it or not, we are all concerned with that world, and I suppose that's why I read the magazine.

In the May 1992 issue, I came across two recent discoveries that changed the way I looked at everything — at least for a while. In their monthly column called "Breakthroughs in science, technology, and medicine", I found a brief piece titled "A Drop of Violence". It begins with a quotation by a mechanical engineer by the name of Lorenz Sigurdson from the University of Alberta in Edmonton. "We are," Dr. Sigurdson says, "surrounded in the world by turbulence." I expected that he would then go on to illustrate his point by referring to any number of recent headlines about the breakup of the Soviet Union or the chaos in world economic conditions, but, no, instead, he was referring to some research that he and others had been doing taking high-speed photographs of color-stained water drops falling into a pool. It is the resulting splashes that represent to Dr. Sigurdson a form of turbulence. Nearby there are three color photos of a single splash taken only thousandths of a second apart. It is Dr. Sigurdson's thesis that this small-scale turbulence is remarkably similar to turbulence on a larger scale.

He has discovered, in fact, that one of those pictures of a splash looks surprisingly like a picture of a nuclear explosion *if* — and this is the clincher — *if* you look at the picture of the explosion upside down. And there, sure enough, next to the three photos of the splashing drop is an upside-down picture of a 1957 nuclear explosion. And, yes, indeed, one of the water drop photos does look like the upside-down blast.

Well, I wanted time to think about all of this before coming to any conclusions, so I read on in my May issue. And there, a few pages later, I came across a second unsettling discovery. This time it concerned a small fossil sea animal that is causing a turbulence of sorts in the world of paleontologists, amongst whom is the prominent Harvard biologist Stephen Jay Gould.

The controversy is over a bizarre looking creature that has been known to science for some time. It apparently roamed the ocean floors of Cambrian seas over 500 million years ago. It has been given the name Hallucigenia, which seems almost perfect. As the article goes on to say,

Hallucigenia is believed to have walked along on seven pairs of long spikes and to have had a row of wavy tentacles along its back. The photo of a fossil Hallucigenia does look very much like something from science fiction.

The article states that Dr. Gould has theorized that 600 million years ago there was an explosion of similarly strange animal forms at a time when multi-celled animals, like Hallucigenia, were just beginning to develop. Most of these forms, Gould says, became extinct simply by chance, thus leaving only the thirty or so phyla that evolved into all the animals on earth today. Further, Gould believes that if we were to run through pre-history again, chance would probably select a different set of basic forms for survival, leading to a totally different kind of life on earth. And we humans might not even exist in that world.

Now, finally, we come to the crux of the story. Fossil creatures have recently been discovered in China that scientists describe as closely related to Hallucigenia. But what these new fossils suggest is that we and Stephen Jay Gould may have been looking at the old, familiar Hallucigenia upside down. If we just turn the picture over, the scientists say, we shall see that Hallucigenia doesn't really look so bizarre after all — but very much, well, at least somewhat, like a familiar centipede. So they now say that there may have been no explosion of life forms at all 500 million years ago, and evolution didn't have lots of different choices that vanished by chance. And Stephen Jay Gould? Well, he's not convinced.

After reading all this I concluded that the water drop engineer from Edmonton and the Hallucigenic people were really onto something. Looking at things upside down can open new worlds for all of us. Why just the other day I punched into my pocket calculator the number 113440 — that's right, 113440. And to my astonishment, when I turned the calculator upside down, I discovered those numbers now looked very much like the words "Oh, hell". It must mean something. Perhaps I'll do an article for *Discover* magazine.

What's That?

Lake Turkana lies in the harsh volcanic country in the northwest corner of Kenya in East Africa. The lake is about 170 miles long and at its widest point it is about thirty miles across. Its northernmost bays and marshes lie in Ethiopia, forming the delta of the Omo River that rises 700 miles further north.

The lake is named after the Turkana tribe, a cattle-raising people who inhabit the country between the lake's western shore and Kenya's boundary with Sudan on the north and with Uganda on the west.

Earlier it was known as Lake Rudolph, dating back to the year 1888 when a German geographer by the name of Count Samuel Teleki became the first European to see the great body of water. He named Lake Rudolph after the son of the Austrian Emperor Franz Joseph, and the name continued to be used until shortly after Kenya's independence in 1963 when it was officially changed to Turkana. Teleki had walked the lake's shoreline taking notes on the geology of the area.

Seventy-nine years later, after Teleki's name had long since been buried beneath the sands of history, a small aircraft flying north from Nairobi to the Omo River valley in Ethiopia was forced to change its course eastward because of severe thunderstorms along the western shore of Lake Turkana. The single passenger aboard that flight was Richard Leakey, the then twenty-three-year-old son of the famous anthropological team of Louis and Mary Leakey. Richard was returning from a week in Nairobi to rejoin an American expedition of which he was part that was searching for prehistoric human remains along the Omo River.

From the window of the aircraft, Richard could see below him beds of sediments whose ancient stratification had been revealed by the erosive power of the countless streams along the lake's edge that come to life during Kenya's annual monsoon rains.

Richard could read the meaning of those exposed sediments sandwiched between layers of volcanic ash. He knew they represented a perfect place to look for the remains of early humans. Within weeks, he was back on the lake's eastern shore — this time in a helicopter he had chartered from the American expedition in Ethiopia. And from the ground he was able to confirm his original conviction about the area's rich potential.

In the following year, 1968, he returned to Turkana's eastern shore with his own expedition, establishing his base camp on a large promontory of land jutting into the lake.

The area was known as Koobi Fora, and in time it would become what has been called "the most abundant and varied assemblage of hominid fossils found so far anywhere in the world."

From the notes of the German geographer Teleki we know that he walked through this same area in 1888. He reported that from the eroded sediments he had gathered some fossil seashells.

When Teleki walked that lakeshore, the idea of the existence of fossilized human remains would have still been a novelty in European thinking. The first acknowledged fossilized human remains had been those of Neandertal man found in 1856 by stone quarriers in the Neander valley of Germany. As an early geologist and as a geographer, Teleki most likely would have known of that event, but he might never have considered the idea of fossil humans in Africa. This raises for me some interesting questions about the nature of scientific discovery.

We tend to think of "discovery" as the process of coming upon something new or unknown. But perhaps "discovery" must first be prepared for in the mind of the discoverer before it can be seen in nature.

So the question here is whether Count Teleki may have walked past exposed fragments of fossil bone and skull without seeing them — because he didn't expect to.

Much of the way in which we perceive the world is based on what I call the three corollaries of environmental perception. The third of these is deceptively simple. "We first must know *that* something is before we can ask *what* something is." Perhaps this may help to explain why Samuel Teleki never "discovered" the fossil bones of early humans at Lake Turkana while Richard Leakey did.

What Happened to Shangri La?

In 1933, when the British author James Hilton published his popular novel *Lost Horizon*, he made plausible for many readers the idea that there might exist in some remote part of the world a hidden, fertile valley ringed by massive mountains, snow-covered and impenetrable, within which a small and deeply religious community lived simply and in harmony with their environment. Hilton located his "lost horizon" somewhere in the Himalayas and he named it Shangri La. Today, although Hilton's book has been forgotten by many, the name Shangri La still touches a responsive chord in our imagination. It stands as a metaphor for everything that is remote and mysterious as well as desirable — a kind of Asian garden of Eden.

In 1933, the Nepalese capital of Kathmandu was virtually unknown to the West. Because of its remoteness and inaccessibility, it became fused in the imagination of many with the mythical world of Shangri La. Fascinating reports from 18th- and 19th-century explorers, travelers, and missionaries helped to confirm this image.

A British traveler to Kathmandu 200 years ago described the valley as having ". . . as many temples as houses and more idols than there are people".

Out of such reports there emerged an image of a world very different from ours — one that was based on a fusion of ancient Hindu and Buddhist beliefs of which the West was almost completely ignorant. It was a world in which material things were seen as illusory, and spiritual concerns were perceived as the ultimate reality.

Between 1846 and 1950, Nepal remained isolated from the outside world, governed by an oligarchy of powerful and wealthy princes known as the Ranas. Then in 1951, King Tribuvan, the grandfather of the present king, claimed his hereditary title to the throne and overthrew the Ranas.

Under his rule, Nepal gradually opened its doors to the West, first to restricted mountain climbing expeditions in the '50s and '60s, and gradually to the ordinary visitor. In 1955, Nepal was admitted to the United Nations, and in 1965, the first road was built to link Kathmandu with the outside world of India.

By the early 1970s when I first traveled to Nepal, Kathmandu was changing rapidly. It had become a haven for Western hippies. Marijuana and hashish were available everywhere. Young people from Holland and Germany, France, England, and America were everywhere as well. A few of them were attracted to Hinduism while others became practicing Buddhists. Some came simply because it was fashionable to do so. And others entered on the disastrous quest through drugs for that mythical, hidden valley that they had failed to find in Kathmandu.

Today Kathmandu must rank among the most polluted cities of the world. Its burgeoning population of motorcycle rickshaws, private cars, taxis, and motor bikes all burn a poorly refined, low-octane gasoline imported from India and fortified with lead to aid combustion. By eleven o'clock on most mornings, the exhaust from these vehicles, coupled with the diesel fumes from the poorly tuned engines of innumerable buses and trucks, makes the air unbreathable. The World Health Organization, whose standards for drinkable water permit one cell of coliform bacteria per hundred milliliters of water, has found during the monsoon season in Kathmandu as many as 4,800 cells of coliform per hundred milliliters.

Agricultural pesticides such as BHC and DDT are in common use by local farmers in the Kathmandu valley, and in recent years local fishermen have augmented their catch by dumping these same pesticides in the many rivers near the city. They have no idea of why the fish are killed, but the poisoned fish bring good prices in the local markets. The fishermen, themselves, who often eat their own catch, have shown increasing signs of nerve damage.

I doubt if Kathmandu was ever Shangri La, but it was clearly very different from what it has become today. What we call progress has changed forever the face of the city and the lives of its people. Certainly in material ways some of them are, as we say, "better off". But I'm not sure what such progress does to mind and spirit. So when I hear the name Kathmandu, I don't think of the lost world of Shangri La, nor do I think of the shiny new motorbikes, nor of the video recorders on sale in the electronics section of the supermarket. Instead I recall some lines near the end of an early poem by T. S. Eliot. He wrote:

> I am moved by fancies that are curled
> Around these images and cling,
> The notion of some infinitely gentle,
> Infinitely suffering thing.

Uphill or Downhill in Nepal?

In May of 1993, I traveled to the tiny kingdom of Nepal. I had been there in 1987, and before that in 1973. As with everywhere in the world, changes are coming to Nepal. It is impossible to predict with any certainty where those changes will lead.

Nepal is a country the size of Maine, New Hampshire, Vermont, and Massachusetts. Its population is estimated to be about twenty-two million as compared to the approximately nine million people who live in the equivalent area of New England.

Nepal is shaped as a narrow rectangle some 500 miles long from east to west and a little more than 100 miles wide from south to north. In that short width the land rises from about 500 feet above sea level in the south to over 29,000 feet at the summit of Mt. Everest. It is not a steady rise in elevation but rather a staggering series of ups and downs in which an automobile would be useless. Even today, most of Nepal is accessible only on foot.

The vast range of the Himalayas that stretches from

Bhutan in the east to Afghanistan in the west forms a 500-mile wall along Nepal's northern border with Tibet — a wall that has served for centuries as a political and physical boundary between north and south. Tiny Nepal is like a vital cushion of cartilage that lies between the huge bones of India and China. And because everyone wants that cushion to remain intact, China and India both compete for Nepal's favor with various aid programs. But the help does not stop there.

In 1987, I was told that forty-three separate agencies, both national and international, were working in Nepal solely on the problems of deforestation and soil erosion. The U.S. Peace Corps is providing teachers and aiding in the development of small business. Canada, Switzerland, Germany, and Holland are helping in road construction, the establishment of a school of engineering, and the development of hydro-power, dairy production, and cottage industries. Japan, the largest donor of overseas aid to Nepal, has devoted its efforts to improved medical care in rural areas.

In short, with millions and millions of dollars of foreign aid flowing in each year, Nepal seems like a country in danger of being helped to death — the death of its own ancient and varied cultures.

With the increased exposure to Western technology, there is a rising demand by Nepalis for video cameras and recorders, motorcycles, radios, and television sets. Shops renting video cassettes are now everywhere in Kathmandu. On an earlier trip to Nepal I recall watching a weekly series on television of the British actress Joan Hickson in her BBC television role as Agatha Christie's Miss Marple — brought to its viewers in English by courtesy of the Himal Cement Company.

And then there is tourism.

In 1961, there were about 6,200 overseas visitors to Nepal. This year [1999] there will be close to 700,000. Many of them will be from the West. Some will come to walk in the mountains to get away from the pressures of business and urban life. Others will be drawn to Nepal because of its ancient and still meaningful religious traditions, or because of its history and its art. They will visit the medieval towns of the Kathmandu valley and the many Hindu temples and Buddhist shrines. Some will develop an interest in Buddhist philosophy or will be attracted to Tibetan medicine and its very different approach to the meaning of illness. Others will become involved with Nepal's many Tibetan refugees in their struggle for their country's independence from China.

And yet in all of this there is a strange irony. For while overseas aid and Western technology are creating in Nepalis that insatiable hunger for material things, many Westerners themselves are drawn to Nepal by a different hunger — one that is perhaps best described by the word "spiritual".

Is this fascination with each other's worlds simply an

illustration of the old adage that "the grass is always greener" elsewhere, or is it something deeper? Are we in the West beginning to recognize the limits of satisfaction that come with success in the material world? Do the Nepalis wish to imitate the West because their exposure to us has led them to no longer value the very aspects of their culture that attract us to them? It almost seems today that people of the West and East are hurtling to embrace each other's worlds, and yet neither one speaks to the other about the meaning of what is being lost or gained.

Is Small Really Beautiful?

Have you ever wondered what the world would be like if we could solve the worst of its environmental problems? Certainly, thoughtful people everywhere are making the attempt to address such issues. Consider the United Nations Conference on Environment and Development that was held in Rio de Janiero in June of 1992. Thirty thousand people from more than 150 countries met to discuss a wide variety of crucial environmental issues and to celebrate the twentieth anniversary of the First World Conference on the Human Environment held in 1972 at Stockholm, Sweden.

Although certainly some valuable consciousness raising takes place at such conferences and a number of resolutions are made, it is not often that there are major changes in the world's behavior. Conferences are just not like that.

But for the moment, let's consider a very different scenario. Let's imagine that we are all there in Rio and it is June of '92. The conference has been running for several days. There have been countless speeches warning about dwindling resources, vanishing species, global warming, and toxic waste — speeches that parade before us the five horsemen of the environmental apocalypse: greed, ignorance, and necessity, followed by destruction, and death.

Imagine, then, after days of dire predictions, that the Director General of the conference announces that on the following morning at nine o'clock, there will be an emergency plenary session with an important announcement that could very well change the future of our planet. Imagine the response and the buzz of speculation about what it all means.

By eight o'clock the following morning, the main conference hall is jammed. Special amplifying equipment has been set up with loudspeakers in every available space, and people are sitting outdoors on the ground, on entrance steps, or in crowded hallways, waiting and talking quietly. Promptly at nine o'clock, the Director General of the conference briefly announces that Lobsang Gyatso from the Autonomous Republic of Tibet will speak. A small gray-haired man, slightly stooped, begins to move slowly from the rear of the conference hall toward the podium. Some few people along the aisle see that he is wearing the long maroon robe of a Tibetan monk. Still fewer people know him as a specialist in herbal medicine who has spent years in studying the life-enhancing properties of different plants.

Then in a soft voice — so soft that the delegates hold their breath to listen — he announces that in 1989 on a trip into western Tibet, near the holy mountain Kailas, he had discovered a rare plant containing a mixture of complex and unfamiliar chemicals. He describes how, with the assistance of colleagues in Europe, the chemicals were analyzed and synthesized early in 1992. In the form of a pill, he explains, the chemical has a profound impact on human perception. He expresses his conviction that by taking the pill we would solve overnight the myriad environmental problems facing the human race.

The delegates are stunned. Immediately following Lobsang Gyatso's talk, the conference steering committee meets in special session. A proposal is made and ratified. The representatives of the world's nations unanimously agree that on August 1st at twelve noon Greenwich time the World Health Organization will supervise the swallowing of one of those special pills by each person on earth. Worldwide unified action is a prime condition of the experiment's success.

August 1st arrives. Precisely at noon, after a nightmare of logistical complications has been overcome, everyone on earth swallows a pill. And then what happens? Immediately all humans shrink to a height of six inches, and everything that humans have ever made — the Pyramids, the Parthenon, the cities and the skyscrapers, the industries and the superhighways — all shrink to a similar scale. What remains as it was is everything we now call nature — the mountains, the forests, the rivers, the arable land, the mineral resources, and the reserves of fossil fuel.

Suddenly population no longer poses a threat in relation to the availability of resources. There is enough land for everyone, and farmland enough to feed us all. An ear of corn that was once eight inches long now stands over the head of the tallest human, with enough kernels to feed a family for a week. A comfortably sized house would cover 250 square feet instead of 3,000. Think of the savings in building materials! And a full-sized car would be sixteen inches long. Think of the fuel economy!

Air pollution would be dramatically reduced. People in the state of Nevada might be lured to California by advertisements for cheap land given to enterprising pioneers who want to help settle its now vast wilderness areas. And then Nevada could safely become the entire nation's dump for toxic waste.

Sure there'd be difficulties, but the military with its small but sophisticated weapons could help cope with the neighborhood dogs or the urban rat population. It is true that mosquitoes would become a whole new environmental problem, but it wouldn't be all bad for everyone. Responding to this scenario, a student of mine once said, his eyes brightening and with a wistful smile on his face, "But think of the surfing!"

Ridiculous? Of course. But just imagine that we could discover some way to diminish our impact on the environment and at the same time dramatically multiply the resources available for human use. The important question is: *Then* how would we behave?

Knowing what we know now we would first certainly give a sigh of relief, but then what? Why would we exercise restraint if there were no physical need to do so, at least for many, many generations? As soon as our present close encounter with limits was over, would we tend to go back to business as usual — to a world in which "unrestrained growth" and "development" were the buzz words of every political candidate? Perhaps your answer will depend on how you see human nature. I find myself wondering whether the so-called environmental crisis may not be the most important opportunity that our species has had. It forces us to a new level of awareness of our relation with our surroundings and asks us to reexamine the connection between the world outside us and the world inside. And maybe it is because the stakes are so high and the time is so short that that process may be more effective than any pill in changing not only our perception but, more importantly, our behavior.

How Much is Too Much?

Some years ago when I was working in central India, I learned that a team of Americans from the U.S. Forest Service and from our Fish and Wildlife Service had been invited by the town fathers of the city of Bombay (called Mumbai, today) to advise them on the establishment of a natural area along the banks of the small river or creek that separates Bombay from the Indian mainland.

Prior to the arrival of European colonial powers in India — the Portuguese in the late 15th century and the British a bit later on — the area that was later named Bombay consisted of some seven islands that were separated from each other only at high tide. The British influence in Bombay really began after the city was given to England's King Charles II in 1662 as part of the dowry of his young Portuguese bride, Princess Catherine of Braganza. Thereafter, King Charles rented Bombay to the British East India Company for the sum of ten pounds a year — in gold.

It was during the time of the British Raj in India, in the

latter half of the 19th century, that the tidal lands separating the islands of Bombay were drained and filled to create the modern city. But the creek remains and today still attracts many species of migratory waterfowl that migrate south in the winter from Siberia, Mongolia, and Tibet down into southern India.

The project that the town fathers had in mind for the American team included the reclamation of the creek and the creation along its banks of a series of public parks and gardens.

The study team's first discovery was that the water of the creek contained no dissolved oxygen whatever and might better have been described as a dark viscous fluid rather than anything resembling water. Yet they believed that problem could be solved by technology. It was further upstream that the real stumbling block to the project lay. There the creek passed through an area of some 250 acres that the study team in their report described as possibly "one of the worst slums in Asia".

Placed in the more familiar context of my home area of Vermont, those 250 acres would represent the area of a moderate-sized dairy farm. One of my neighbors up the road has a farm just about that size. On it he grows corn and hay for his cows. From its woodlands he harvests saw logs and firewood and makes maple syrup. The one house on the property is occupied by him and his wife and their two children. A hired man lives in a trailer. But that same

250-acre area of Bombay was occupied by over 200,000 people. There was no building over one story high, and there were no sewage facilities of any kind. In order for the proposed reclamation project to have any chance of success, the study team felt the 200,000 people would have to be relocated. The problem was that there was no place for them to go.

Recently, I read in the *Wall Sreet Journal* that international environmental organizations consider world population to be *the* critical issue in the coming decade. No other single factor, the article said, places an equivalent stress on the resources on our planet. The National Academy of Sciences is quoted as saying that population growth is "the single biggest driver of atmospheric pollution".

What is at stake here, however, is not just resources or clean air. It is something much harder to measure — something that can only be described as the quality of life. And of course the definition of that quality will be different for each person.

But even as I write, there is a silent, dynamic force at work that will affect the future quality of life for the people of all nations. For as you near the end of reading this approximately four-and-a-half-minute essay, there will be 720 more people on earth than when you began.

During a one-hour radio or television special devoted to the pros and cons of a woman's right to choice in giving birth, 9,800 more people are added. And two and a half days from now, the number of people on earth will have increased by the equivalent of Vermont's entire population of 604,000.

Is it possible that our inability to plan for our collective future is the result of some inherent flaw in human perception? In so many aspects of our lives we seem unable to understand that what is enough can only be measured against what is too much. The danger with the issue of population is that by the time we understand what is too much it may be too late to do anything about it. And then whatever we call the quality of life will be meaningful only as history.

Land's End?

In 1927, Charles Lindbergh made his solo flight across the Atlantic Ocean from New York to Paris. Since that time, one could say that the world has shrunk. Certainly the increasing speed of aircraft has made traveling long distances much shorter in time.

But the world has shrunk in other ways as well. In 1927, there were about twenty acres of land area for each man, woman, and child then living on our planet. Today, there are six acres for each person on the earth. It sounds like quite a lot of land, really — six acres. But if each of our six-acre pieces contained a representative portion of earth's different land forms, it would mean that four acres out of every six would consist of desert, polar ice and snow, high mountains, and tropical rain forest. Now although we realize that people can and do live in such environments, we also realize that they are marginal acres for the development of what today we mean by civilization. So it is on the remaining two acres out of six that almost all human activity is concentrated on the planet.

On a little over half an acre of those two we grow all the foods that we consume directly, as well as all the grains for our domestic livestock. On that same land, we grow all our cash crops — the coffee, the cotton, the tea, the sisal, and tobacco. And today we must include among the most valuable of such crops the poppies, the coca, and the marijuana. On the remaining acre and a quarter or so are the great grazing lands of Australia, Africa, and North and South America, as well as the important temperate forests of Canada and North America, of Russia, Europe, and Scandinavia.

It is also on these same two acres that we build all our homes and businesses, our industries and cities, our highways, shopping centers, and our schools and hospitals.

The dramatic change that has taken us from twenty acres of land for each person in 1927 to six acres today in the year 2001 does indeed make it seem as though our earth has shrunk. But of course it is we who have grown. In 1950, the earth's population increased at the rate of 1.6%. This year it is projected that the rate of increase will be about 1.4%. The rate of increase in 1950 added 40 million to the plant's population. This year, however, the increase is expected to be about 86 million people — even at the lower rate.

Now count out loud: "one thousand one, one thousand two". In the space of those two seconds, five more people will have been added to our population. "One thousand one, one thousand two." Five more. And this is after deaths!

Perhaps one of those five is born in your home town. By the time he or she is twelve years old, one billion more people will have been added to the total population.

Now we know that a billion is a very large number of anything, but at the same time it is very difficult for us to fully appreciate its magnitude. How can a billion be made more comprehensible? Most often we hear this number referred to in terms of national budgets or military spending. So let's translate it first into dollars.

If you were extremely wealthy and also very long-lived, and if you had had the opportunity to spend a thousand dollars every day on anything you wanted, and you had started at the time of Christ's birth and continued your buying spree each day for fifty-two weeks a year until today in 2001, how much more than a billion dollars would you have spent? Well, the answer is that you wouldn't have spent anywhere near a billion dollars. You would still have nearly 739 years in which to spend a thousand dollars a day before you reached a billion. That, incidentally, is another way of looking at the approximate cost of two Stealth bombers.

But now back to people. If we increased earth's population by a thousand people every day, it would take us more than 2,700 years to add an additional billion people. At present rates of growth, we are going to add that billion people in the next twelve years!

Something Missing

In an earlier essay, I referred to a conference that I had been invited to attend in Caracas, Venezuela, in February of 1992. It was the fourth time in as many decades that the world's nations had gathered to consider the state of our planet's national parks and protected areas. It was hosted jointly by the government of Venezuela and the World Conservation Union, a multinational, nongovernmental organization, headquartered in Switzerland. Over the course of twelve days, some 2,000 delegates from approximately 156 countries participated in workshops and symposia dealing with a staggering diversity of topics.

One comes away from such an experience with a mixture of reactions. Perhaps of greatest meaning is the opportunity to pick up the thread of old friendships that in some cases may go back over more than thirty years. One learns, too, about what others are doing, and hears of the efforts of so many who are trying to make a difference despite the obstacles — obstacles that are economic, or political, or simply the result of human ignorance and greed.

In a slightly lighter vein, one is immensely appreciative at such gatherings that the spoken word is "biodegradable". How fortunate it is that words don't linger in the air until they are emptied of meaning and then fall to the ground and lie there waiting for someone to sweep them up and throw them away. The number of words spoken by 2,000 people meeting for twelve days is overwhelming.

Perhaps for me, the most memorable aspects of that conference were not in its content but in the unanticipated and peripheral events that in retrospect color the entire experience.

A few days before the conference began, the international press reported an attempt by the military to overthrow the Venezuelan government. In reality it turned out that the effort was not so much to get rid of the government as to assassinate the president, Carlos Andres Perez. Within a matter of hours, troops loyal to the president defeated the forces responsible for the attempt on his life and captured the leaders. As the conference opened, their fate was unclear. One heard talk that they were to be executed.

On the first morning, the huge complex of conference buildings surrounding the Caracas Hilton hotel was swarming with military and police. Young men in high black leather boots held tightly to the leashes of powerful and unpleasant looking Doberman pinschers. Clubs, semi-automatic pistols, and handcuffs hung from the heavy black belts the young men wore. Slung over their shoulders were automatic rifles. Some of the men wore fingerless black gloves, the bulging knuckles revealing the lead shot that lined the insides. Carefully, they checked the green identity card of each delegate.

By the time President Perez arrived at the huge conference hall to deliver his opening address, the more than 2,000 people were already seated. He was preceded into the hall by some eight or ten plainclothes security guards. They took their places across the front of the wide stage, standing with legs apart, hands at their sides, facing the audience. They remained there during the president's speech, their eyes scanning the auditorium for any abrupt or inappropriate movement that might contain a threat.

The president welcomed us to Venezuela and spoke of the beauty of his country's national parks and of their important contribution both to environmental quality and to the tourist industry. His speech seemed, in that setting, somehow incongruous. From the back of the room, a mixed chorus sang the Venezuelan national anthem. And then the president left surrounded by his guards. He had demonstrated that he was still very much in power.

Later that morning, I talked with one of the delegates from the United States National Park Service. He was a young Navajo from Arizona, a park interpreter at Canyon de Chelly, one of the most important of Navajo sacred areas. He had come to the conference to represent not only the National Park Service but the Navajo tribe as well. He

explained to me that a special ceremony had been performed for him by the Navajo elders before he left Arizona
to sanction and to bless his journey to Venezuela. He had
come there, as he said, on a "vision quest". On his return to
America, he was to relate to them what he had seen and
learned at the Caracas conference.

"I was at the opening of the conference this morning," he
said, "and I heard the president of Venezuela speak. Why is
it," he asked, "that when the nations of the world gather at
such an important occasion there is no opening ritual or
ceremony that speaks to something other than the *physical*
needs of man?" In the directness of his question he touched
on something that I was to find missing throughout the
entire conference.

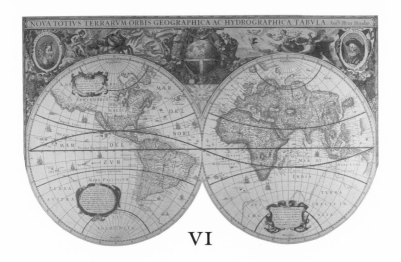

VI

From Africa to India
— Five Tales

Four of the stories that follow grew out of the many years
I spent working and traveling in East Africa, an experience
that shaped my life between the ages of thirty and sixty.
Then in the 1970s, I interspersed my African travels with a
series of trips to India as a consultant with the International Division of the U.S. Park Service.

I find I return in my thoughts almost daily to Africa and
India, not so much in nostalgia as in wonder at the dura-
bility of the immense tapestry of experiences woven during those years.

A Garden Far Away

"And where was that photograph taken?" The speaker was one of the last visitors to the exhibition that gray October Sunday. Initially my attention was caught by the care with which she examined each of my pictures. Of the three or four hundred people who had attended the open house at the small museum, most had passed rapidly through the two rooms where the photographs were hung, on their way to other exhibits. The more familiar photographic subjects — a weathered New Hampshire barn, an evening seascape on the Massachusetts coast, the flame of autumn leaves on a Vermont hillside — had elicited pleasant sounds of recognition. The less familiar scenes from Nepal and Africa had provoked few comments. So her question came as a surprise.

"That was taken in Ethiopia," I replied.

She was standing some distance from the picture, her folded eyeglasses held upright against pursed lips. Abruptly she snapped the glasses open, put them on with both hands and advanced with lowered head to within a few inches of the photograph. She studied it not as a picture but almost as a piece of fabric, almost as though she were examining it for flaws. I found myself irritated by her manner.

Still carefully studying the picture, she spoke again. "I assume you are the photographer, aren't you? Otherwise you wouldn't be loitering about so."

The directness of her comment made me smile. Until that moment I hadn't considered how my presence there might be viewed. Each of us has a different way of interpreting even the most common event.

"Tell me about that small figure in the foreground," she went on. "Its body is so smooth and black that it looks more like an ebony wood-carving."

"It's a young Galla boy," I said, "looking after his father's cattle."

"Cattle?" she asked, turning toward me for the first time. "I don't see any cattle."

"His brothers and sisters had led them away from the water hole before I took the picture."

"The surface of the water is unusual," she said. "The way it reflects the color of the trees and the distant hills behind it gives it a texture like gold brocade."

"I've never looked at it that way before," I said appreciatively.

"What are those brown balls hanging from the trees?"

"Nests of weaver birds," I replied. "And the trees are acacias."

She stepped back from the photograph and removed her glasses. "It's a kind picture, gentle and peaceful. I like the way the branch of that big tree in the foreground arches over the little black child. It provides a marvelous frame for the water hole, the trees, and the hills. Does the mountain have a name?"

"Yes," I said. "It's called Mount Fantale."

"Would you like to know what the picture says to me?" she asked.

"I'd be very interested," I said, and I meant it.

"It reminds me of what the Garden must have been like — the first garden, before we came to know so much, before science, before technology, and before the coming of what we have the audacity to call progress. We human beings have become a displaced species because we've tried to separate ourselves from our origins in nature. And all we've succeeded in doing is making everything more complicated. That child knows nothing of these things, and I envy him his innocence. That's what it says to me."

"It's a very thoughtful comment," I said.

"Isn't that what you intended to say when you took the picture?"

I hesitated, not knowing quite how to respond. "I'm not sure I can answer that," I replied.

"Well, I'm certain you must have had something like that

in mind, otherwise the picture wouldn't have come out as it did. I can see that just by looking at it."

She snapped open the large purse hanging from her left arm, deposited her eyeglasses inside, and then with one or two comments about my exhibit, thanked me and left the room.

I turned back to the photograph of the little boy beneath Mount Fantale. The room was empty now as I thought about her comments and especially her last question: "Isn't that what you intended to say when you took the picture?" I recalled each of the events leading up to my taking of the picture. Words from another context came back to me: "Each of us has a different way of interpreting even the most common event."

It must have been almost midday when the Land Rover in which I was traveling approached the water hole. It lay just to the side of the narrow dirt track. Four young children had finished watering a small herd of zebu cattle, and as the emaciated animals moved slowly across the road in front of us, we stopped to let them pass. I climbed out with my camera in the hope of a photograph that I knew was there somewhere. As I did so, another vehicle arrived from the opposite direction, its horn blowing insistently. It, too, was stopped by the cattle. In an area as remote as this, such an encounter was uncommon, so it was out of curiosity that I turned toward the other vehicle as its occupants climbed out. A dark, burly European was the first to emerge. On his hip hung a semi-automatic pistol in an open holster. Behind him came three Ethiopians, each with an automatic rifle. Bandoleers of bullets were slung crossways over their chests, and from their belts dangled hand grenades like small gray pineapples. The European waved at me and began shouting at the children in Amharic to clear the track of cattle. The children, clearly frightened, buzzed like insects about the legs of the slowly moving animals, stinging them with stones and sticks. The European had noticed my camera and called to me in broken English, "You want picture cattle?"

I think he was ready to stop their progress on my behalf — not from any inherent interest in photography but simply because it would have provided him with another opportunity to exercise his authority.

"No," I called back, and then, without thinking: "I'm more interested in the children."

That was all he needed. In a matter of seconds, following his barked order, his men had herded the four children together into a terrified little huddle. It wasn't exactly what I had in mind for a photograph.

"Would the tallest boy be willing to stand near that tree by the water hole?" I asked.

Grabbing the boy by the shoulder, the European spun

him round and marched him over to the place I had indicated. "Stand there," he commanded, or something that had the same effect.

Rather reluctantly, I raised my camera. The boy squirmed like an insect newly pinned on a collecting board. There was a long silence — then the obtrusive mechanical clank of the camera shutter filled the hot, empty space of the surrounding country. The boy's body jerked and wriggled while his feet remained rooted to that one spot.

I walked toward him, made some inadequate remark of thanks, reached into my pocket and brought out a coin. In a swift motion, it disappeared from my hand into his, and then into his mouth. His companions stood at a distance. I don't know if they saw the coin.

By now the cattle had crossed the track. I exchanged a few words with the European. He had, it seems, been in Ethiopia for years, training pilots for the Emperor's air force. One always traveled in these remote areas with an armed guard, he said. Ambush was a common occurrence. By whom and for what reason was a subject I didn't explore. We left to travel in opposite directions.

That is the context of the photograph. It contains many elements not revealed by the picture itself, elements which greatly affect its meaning for me. Many things within the picture also affect its meaning, but only if one is conscious of their implications.

Behind the boy rises Mount Fantale — a sleeping but still smoldering volcano. Its rich lava slopes once covered by heavy forests have been stripped for firewood, then grazed by cattle and goats. With the cutting of the forests, the capacity of the mountain slopes to hold water has rapidly diminished, and the underground springs that once provided water year round to places many miles from the mountain are drying up. Now the water holes are fewer, and their supplies fluctuate with the seasons.

Deforestation and overgrazing have caused the land between the water holes and the mountain to become increasingly desiccated. The invading thornbush, resistant to drought and to damage by livestock, is changing the open savannah to a wasteland.

The water holes are the natural habitat for the African freshwater snail. In combination with the human wastes that foul the waters, the snails become hosts to millions of microscopic flukes — the carriers of the crippling human disease known as bilharzia, or schistosomiasis.

So for me the picture offers no appealing alternative to the world that modern man has created. Instead it makes me thoughtful about something Carl Jung once wrote:

> Every problem, therefore, brings the possibility of a widening of consciousness, but also the necessity of saying goodbye to childlike unconsciousness and trust in nature. . . . It is the sacrifice of the merely natural man, of the unconscious,

ingenuous being whose tragic career began with the eating of the apple in Paradise.

Sometimes I find myself wondering if the little boy is still alive.

The Man with the Sun in His Hand

He has become such an abstraction to me that I never think of him as anything but "The Man with the Sun in His Hand". I don't think I ever knew his real name. Perhaps if it became important enough, I could find out. Sometimes I imagine going on such a quest — not so much in an attempt to relive an experience as simply to see if he's still there. In Africa, the passage of twenty-eight years can mean nothing — and everything.

I would begin my search by hiring a car in Nairobi. Then, heading out in the early morning along Uhuru Highway, I would turn west toward Nairobi National Park. The road runs past a new subdivision of flats, past Wilson Airport and the police barracks, by the main park entrance and the cemetery across the road. Then it drops down through heavy forest, rises again into more open country, and at this point, I would turn left off the main road and drive south toward the Ngong Hills. The chainlink fence that forms the west boundary of the national park would be on my left. I would pass the driveways leading to Colonel

Mervyn Cowie's old house and the Banda Hotel. The suburban development of Nairobi would be behind me now, and I would find myself among the small *shambas* (farms) and tin-roofed huts that have sprung up indiscriminately along the Ngong Road in recent years. The track begins to climb, and the lovely shapes of the Ngong Hills slowly appear. At the high point where the road crosses the shoulder of the hills, I would stop and get out as I have done on so many other occasions. Even on the hottest of days, there is always a breeze on that ridge.

Looking behind me toward Nairobi, I would see the gray halo of smog that hovers over the city these days. In the opposite direction, looking south, I would see the empty hills rippling down and away in the blue distance toward Olorgesailie and Lake Magadi — no smog there, only thorn bush and the barren hills with their tumbled outcroppings of rock.

Such perspectives offer an endless opportunity for metaphor. To stand there Janus-like, listening to the wind whistling through the thorn bush, is to be in a doorway between two worlds, one very new and the other immeasurably old. One almost finds oneself momentarily inclined toward prophecy. Although that distant city, shimmering in the morning sun, may well represent the promise of the future, it may be that the desolate bush and rock-strewn hills provide the more accurate vision of things to come. Standing in such a place, one cannot help but glimpse in the distant heat haze the ruins of other shimmering cities that now lie buried beneath the African landscape. It is a land where the temporal and the timeless are inseparably interwoven.

The track that leads steeply down from the high ridge of the Ngongs twists first to the right and then drops in a sweeping left-hand curve before it straightens for the long gradual descent toward the Tanzanian border.

On leaving the ridge of the hills, one enters a different world. It is true that there are reminders of today's world — the small *duka* (shop) on the left of the track with its rusted Pepsi Cola sign hanging like a battered but still garish badge against the otherwise uniformly colored landscape. But Nairobi is no longer visible from here, just a herd of giraffe and the hills and the long stretch of country ahead. It is in such country that The Man with the Sun in His Hand lived.

He was an aging Maasai. I visited his *manyatta* (low circular house constructed of cattle dung and sticks) only once and then it was at night. I don't know if I could find it again. I don't even know if it's still there.

One comes across the abandoned *manyattas* of the Maasai in the silent heat of midday. The small dung-covered huts are enclosed by surrounding walls of dry thorn bush that serve as a kind of natural barbed wire to protect the cattle at night from lion and hyena. In time, the thorn bush enclosure is bleached silver by the hot sun, and it is not long before the structure is reclaimed by the African landscape. All that remains are the trampled rings of cattle dung, marking where the enclosures had once been. From the air, the scars of these old *manyattas* look like bomb craters of some long-forgotten war.

The Man with the Sun in His Hand lived in a *manyatta* that lay to the south of the archeological site at Olorgesailie. In the darkness when I first saw it, it seemed more permanent than many Maasai settlements. My recollection is that some of the huts had tin roofs. There may even have been a *duka* near by. If that were so, I could question the shopkeeper about the old man — but I'm not sure how I would begin. To try to describe him would only lead to confusion. He looked like so many other Maasai: tall, flamingo-thin, maybe fifty-five years old. He wore the traditional ochre-colored *shuka* (toga) knotted at the right shoulder, its long hem flapping about his wiry legs — a circle of ivory tusk on his left wrist, and a silver bracelet and one of elephant hair on his right. From his pierced, extended earlobes hung ornaments in the form of diminutive brass bells.

In what way could I distinguish him from others? To say that he was The Man with the Sun in His Hand would certainly set him apart. But it might do the same for me and make further questions futile.

Only one slender possibility would remain by which I might hope to locate him — just one tiny clue. "Do you by any chance know," I might ask the shopkeeper, "if there's an elderly Maasai about, or a family of Maasai, any one of whom may be seen chewing a piece of gum?" It would be a difficult question to ask. It would take courage. But in my imagination I see the eyes of the shopkeeper suddenly brighten with recognition and understanding. "Ndio, bwana. Ndio. Nafahamu kabisa sasa." Now I know who you mean. Oh, yes. You are looking for old OleMolo, the chewing-gum man. He and his family live just there — in that hut beyond the wreck of the old Bedford lorry.

Ridiculous as it all may sound, I am certain that the chewing gum would be my only hope of finding him and learning his name. But then when I reflect a bit on the actuality of such an event, I think it's probably best to forget the whole thing. What, after all, would I say if I were to find him? All I really want to know is if he is still there. I'm not sure why, except that for me, and perhaps for some others who have seen his picture, he has become the embodiment of an idea — not just to do with chewing gum, but something more important. To explain that idea I must go back to the beginning — to that day years ago when he first held the sun in his hand.

Early on that particular morning, along with my two American associates, I entered one of the buildings behind the National Museum in Nairobi and climbed the wooden staircase to Richard Leakey's office. I had called Richard the previous day to ask for his help. I knew we could count on him to listen, to give advice, and, if he were able, to offer assistance. It had been some time since I had sat in his office talking with him about the museum, and it was good to catch up on much that had gone on between visits. He asked what we were up to, and I made what must have seemed a bizarre request. I said that I wanted to find an elderly Maasai whom I could film as he walked through open bush country in the late afternoon. In the process of his journey, I wanted him to "discover" a stone hand-axe lying partly exposed on the ground. I wanted him to pick up his discovery, and, by his contemplation of it, to suggest his concern with its origin and meaning. I wondered if the archeological site at Olorgesailie would be an appropriate place to film such a sequence as I knew that one could find there both Maasai and stone hand-axes.

Richard withdrew the large curved pipe from his mouth, and, with the characteristic patience of one who is used to coping with the unfamiliar, asked us to tell him what it was we thought we were doing. From our earlier phone conversation he knew that we had come to Kenya to work on part of a film project for the U.S. National Park Service. But some elaboration did seem necessary.

I explained that in September of the following year, 1972, the U.S. National Park Service, together with the International Union for the Conservation of Nature in Switzerland, were to act as hosts to delegates from some ninety nations at the Second World Conference on National Parks.

The purpose of this conference, which was to be held at Grand Teton National Park in Wyoming, was to discuss the myriad problems facing the world's park community — problems of economics, resource depletion, education, overcrowding, environmental protection, and so forth. In short, the conference was to be a kind of microcosm of the similar but larger-scale United Nations' Conference on the Human Environment to be held in Stockholm in June of that same year. 1972 was thus to become a benchmark for international environmental concerns.

Our task was to produce a film for the National Parks Conference that would help to provide a perspective on man's relationship with his natural environment. The film would not be concerned with specifics of pollution or population or resource consumption, but rather with the differing human values and attitudes by which the natural world is perceived.

If our film were to have broad use internationally, it could not depend on any particular language to communicate its meaning. Although its sound track might be in several languages, its meaning would have to be contained, not in words, but in visual images.

Our coming to Kenya, I told him, was simply one more step in a long journey. We had already been gathering material in Tunisia, filming the ancient food-production techniques of the Berbers, the camel caravans in the Northern Sahara, and the magnificent ruins of the Roman city of

Dougga where the cobblestone streets still bear the wheel ruts worn by the traffic of chariots from 2,000 years ago. Then on to Ethiopia to film the depletion of the earth in the desperate quest by so many for food, the fantastic moonscape of the Simien Mountains, and the agricultural practices and religious ceremonies of peoples virtually unchanged since Biblical times.

In retrospect, these images formed a kaleidoscope not only of the human environment but of time as well. Sitting in Richard Leakey's office, however, it was impossible to see our work in such a perspective. We were too closely enmeshed in the process itself, and so much lay ahead that could not be foreseen that morning.

It was difficult to explain to Richard my interest in filming a Maasai contemplating a stone axe. I knew that it had to do with a concern with time. The age that separates the Maasai's world of today from that of the stone-axe culture of the ancient lake-shore peoples of Olorgesailie who lived there over 200,000 years ago is far greater than the time that divides London or New York from the world of the Maasai. The length of time alone makes little difference. It is in the rate of change within time that the difference lies.

Standing on the ridge of the Ngong Hills offers the observer a perspective in time, and so too, I thought, might the image of a Maasai contemplating the stone tool of a people who had lived 200,000 years before. It was in Tunisia that I had filmed a desert tribesman seated on the warm sands by his tethered camel in the morning sun. He was carefully tuning his transistor radio to pluck from one of the wavelengths of radiant energy the funeral elegy for Gamal Abdel Nasser being spoken in Cairo, nearly 1,200 miles away.

It was T. S. Eliot who said:

> Time present and time past
> Are both perhaps present in time future
> And time future contained in time past.

I cannot now recall precisely what we said to Richard Leakey that morning, but the upshot of our meeting was that he planned to drive to Olorgesailie in the afternoon to meet us. As he did not want to disturb any of the hand-axes at the site, he said he would bring a selection from the museum. He added that if we arrived a bit early, we could probably locate a Maasai at one of the nearby *manyattas*.

We left for Olorgesailie before noon that day, passing over the Ngong Hills through that beautiful doorway in time. In Nairobi, the day had started out cloudy, and, with filming in mind, I had been concerned about rain. As we drove south, however, more and more blue sky began to appear. Huge fragments of broken cloud cover drifted across the sun, dappling the earth in rapidly moving patterns of brilliant light and shadow.

In East Africa, filming at midday, when the sky is clear and the sun is almost directly overhead, is not very productive. The landscape is for the most part shadowless and undefined. It is in the early morning or late afternoon that the light becomes more interesting. So we had planned to make use of the last two or three hours of daylight at Olorgesailie. Since we needed to find a Maasai and an appropriate setting for the sequence, we wanted an additional couple of hours, and, of course, we looked forward to the opportunity of exploring the archeological site.

The Kenyan in charge of the site had been there for years, and he was both knowledgeable and helpful. We shook hands and exchanged greetings, and he immediately sent one of his men in search of a suitable Maasai elder who might be willing to spend some time working with us later in the afternoon. In a matter of a few minutes, we found an excellent place in which to film, and then, with a bit of time remaining before Richard's arrival, we set off to see the small museum of excavated artifacts and to look at the diggings.

Olorgesailie is a quietly disturbing place. Some of the diggings are carefully preserved under thatched lean-tos so that visitors may view the artifacts as they were revealed *in situ* in the sand and gravel soils.

The area was apparently a prehistoric center for the mass-production of stone tools. Skillfully flaked hand-axes, designed for digging, scraping, and skinning, litter the bare surface of the ground in numbers that are certainly in the hundreds and perhaps even the thousands. The original "factory" for this incredible output was ideally situated for human settlement on the shore of a long-since vanished lake, in an area where there was access to a considerable quantity of workable stone.

Potential "customers" must have come from miles away since the plethora of axes lying about suggests a demand for these tools far beyond the needs of any local population. One cannot but speculate, however, that the market was ultimately saturated. Much to posterity's benefit, a tremendous number of axes were apparently never "sold". On the other hand, it may be that these tools were so easily obtained and of such simple craftsmanship that they were considered merely "throw-aways", much as soft-drink containers are today. Yet the skill with which the finely flaked cutting edges were produced makes it difficult to accept the idea that the tools were disposable. Hand-axes from Olorgesailie would have been invaluable possessions and must have represented a giant stride in the technology of survival.

Although it hardly fits the description of one of those "shimmering cities that lie beneath the thorn bush and tumbled rocks of Africa", Olorgesailie is one of those special places where the passage of time becomes almost tangible. To be the only visitor at the site and to sit by oneself toward evening among the ancient stone tools is a great privilege. The cries of the gray hornbill are carried by the soft wind that rises in the dry valley. Gradually the light fails. The last rays of the sun linger for a few moments on the high peaks of the surrounding mountains, turning them first to gold and then to red as the fire dies.

At such moments, our perspective of ourselves in time and space is altered. We become aware of our diminished importance in the scheme of things. It is a humbling experience and therefore rare — and it is not without benefit.

The arrival of Richard's car brought our exploration of the diggings to an end. He climbed out, carrying a parcel. Then, squatting on the ground, he unwrapped it, and there before him lay three beautifully shaped hand-axes.

One of my assistants, the science consultant to the film project, asked Richard how long it would have taken to make such tools, and what the process might have been like.

Richard looked up with a smile. "If you'd like, I'll show you," he said. Without further comment he disappeared down a steep bank that led toward a dry streambed several hundred yards away.

At that moment the Kenyan in charge pointed behind us. "Eh, tayari, bwana. Maasai anakuja sasa." There, approaching us in the company of the assistant who'd been sent in search of him, was a distinguished looking Maasai. Although he was clearly an elderly man, he walked with the characteristic grace and ease of someone used to covering long distances on foot. There was an exchange of greetings and then a ritual handshake, his left hand supporting his right elbow with the right hand extended in greeting. He had come, he said, to help us make our pictures and would stay as long as we needed him. I thanked him and the assistant, too.

Richard reappeared, clutching a stone in each hand. He squatted on the ground once more. With his left hand on top, he stood the longer of the stones upright in the dust of the car park. Grasping the smaller stone in his right, he hefted it once or twice, turning it over until its balance and position seemed right. Then tilting the upright stone at a slight angle, he struck it a sharp blow near the base. A large flake broke free. He struck again, a little higher — another perfect flake. Without hesitation he proceeded to shape one edge and then the other. In under two minutes, he had transformed the stone into a usable tool with two excellent edges.

He looked up. "There aren't many people who still know how to do this," he said quietly — not immodestly, but simply as a matter of fact. "I learned it from my father. The trick is choosing the proper stones for the axe and for the flaking tool. It's also a bit of a trick in learning how and where to strike to get the right size flake. It's easy to remove too much or too little." He stood up. "Right," he said, "you're all set. I'll leave these tools with you to take back to the museum. I see you've got your Maasai." The old man stood looking at the axes on their cloth wrapping and at the new one Richard had just made. "I'm off," Richard said. "Let me know how it goes with you."

We gathered up the camera gear and set off. Before

Richard's arrival, I'd chosen a place for the filming that lay only a short walk from the archeological site. Its topography was ideal for the scene I wanted to record. The camera could be set up against the bank of an old streambed. From there, the land stretched away for miles in all directions in undulating waves. If the light cooperated, there would be breaks in the clouds and the whole scene would be illuminated by the late afternoon sun. The old Maasai padded silently along on his tire-tread sandals. One of my assistants carried the stone axes and a bulky camera case. The science consultant had the aluminum film box, the stand-by camera, and a heavy tripod. It was a strange group that proceeded in single file to the streambed. The sophisticated camera equipment and the stone hand-axes represented a mingling of tools that bridged 200,000 years and pointed to an end or purpose beyond any conception in the mind of their creators — perhaps even beyond our own conception of why we were there. I wondered how the old Maasai might interpret these things.

He waited patiently as the equipment was set up, as light readings were taken, cameras loaded and checked, battery levels measured. A cloud passed over the face of the declining sun, and in seconds the air grew chilly. This part of the world was turning inexorably toward night. We had at most an hour of usable light remaining.

In my mind, I had been so clear about how I wanted to shoot this sequence that it wasn't until we were ready to begin that I realized how little had been explained to the old Maasai. The stone axes lay on the ground on top of their cloth wrappings. I picked one up and walked over to the Maasai. "Bwana," I asked him, "shoka la mkono hili lina miaka mingapi?" How old do you think this hand-axe is? I realized that the formality of my Tanzanian Swahili must have sounded foreign to him.

"Miaka mingi sana, bwana. Hii ni shoka ya siku zamani za kali sana." It comes from very old times, he said. He apparently knew something of its age, but I wondered how he viewed the man who had made it and what "very old times" meant in his terms. After all, he had watched Richard Leakey make one just a few minutes earlier.

I described how I wanted him to walk toward the camera from the west. When he reached the riverbank, he was to pass along its edge so I could follow him by swinging the camera slowly eastward. That way he could be in full sunlight when he "discovered" the axe. I showed him where we would partially bury it with just an edge protruding. He was to squat down, remove it from the bank, and then, holding it in his hand, he was to examine it closely. For each of my directions, he nodded in understanding and assent. We then made two or three dry runs.

As I took out my light-meter to check the levels once more, a packet of chewing gum fell from the pocket of my vest. I stooped to retrieve it, pulled out a stick, and offered it to the Maasai, saving the last piece for myself. As I opened the wrapper, the old Maasai watched; then he, too, removed the wrapper from his. Somewhat tentatively he placed the stick of gum in his mouth as he had seen me do. We seemed to be silent partners in an activity that had assumed an almost ritualistic importance. The old man closed his jaw once, carefully, and then with his head cocked slightly to one side, he seemed almost to listen to the flavor. He smiled. Then once more he chewed. Then again. His jaw was like a tiny engine that started slowly, increased in speed and, with the flavor of the gum to fuel its operation, settled down to run smoothly and without interruption.

We busied ourselves with burying the stone axe in the bank and removing the extra ones. I slid down the bank to where the camera stood on its tripod. We were ready to begin. I looked up and found that the Maasai was nowhere in sight. "Where's he gone?" I called.

I climbed the bank again. The landscape as far as we could see was deserted. Then we saw the Maasai's head bob up from a depression in the ground 200 yards away. He was walking fast toward the west. "Rob, would you catch up with him," I said, "and get him in position to begin his walk. I'll wave my arm when I want him to start."

Rob set off at a trot. I waited on the bank, hoping to see the distance between them narrow. The old Maasai was three or four hundred yards away and walking fast. As I stood there, I saw that a long thin bank of clouds had formed across the face of the sun. Beneath them the sky on the horizon was clear. Where I was standing was in shadow, but I could see the clouds moving eastward toward me. If more clouds didn't form too fast, it wouldn't be long before the sun would reappear and we would have good light. The Maasai must have been a quarter of a mile away by now. I wondered for a moment if he might simply keep on walking. I couldn't see Rob anywhere. Then the Maasai reached the top of a small rise and stopped. Apparently he was waiting. I saw Rob emerge from the depression, still moving at a trot.

Jumping down to where the camera stood, I swung it into position. Through the viewing system, I could barely locate the figure of the Maasai against the sky. He was standing in darkness silhouetted against the sunlit plains. I saw Rob's outline move to the top of the rise to join him. I locked the tripod head, climbed the bank once more, and waved both arms. Rob waved back and then dropped from sight behind the rise. The old Maasai began to walk.

I brought my eye up against the rubber cup of the camera's viewer, my whole attention focused on the miniature world inside. I heard the whir of the camera motor and watched the tiny figure moving slowly toward me.

As I watched, I had the strange feeling that I was standing in that vast landscape peering into a time machine — one that permitted me to view backward down a long dark corridor. In the light at the end of that corridor I could see a tiny shape moving. Even at that distance, the figure was instantly recognizable. It was a human — a creature walking upright on stick-like legs, moving into the darkness toward some unknown destination. The figure was no longer that of an individual. It was Man himself, emerging from a past beyond memory — out of the gravel soils of the Olduvai Gorge, out of the windswept shores of Lake Turkana and the Omo River — Man the fire-maker, Man the tool-flaker. The glittering surface of that vanished lake danced in the mirage on the horizon. Threads of smoke curled from the cooking fires of the hand-axe people gathered on the shore. Time passed. The upright figure, feared by all creatures, fearful himself of the darkness, walked on. It was only his awareness of himself as Man that separated him from the other animals. His consciousness brought the world to being, naming the trees and grasses, the birds and other animals, conjuring them up by the magic of his words to come forth out of the darkness into the light of his mind, and seeking always still other worlds for his mind to bring into being.

The lake and the cooking fires had vanished over the horizon of time. The figure journeyed on as a small silhouette against the sunlight that followed him as he walked. With each step forward, the edge of darkness was erased. Yet he, himself, moved always in the shadow. Time passed again.

Stretching behind him now in long succession as far as

the eye could see lay the fragments of the great empires of Songhay and Mali, and still farther back, the broken stelae of Axum. In the far distance, one could glimpse the temple of the Lion God amid the ruins of the grassland kingdoms of Naga and Meroe.

Gradually the vision waned, and as the figure approached closer it became that of a solitary nomadic herdsman traveling across the high country of East Africa in the late afternoon. The scene might have been that of today or three hundred years ago. So small a unit of time was meaningless on such a scale. The sunlight still followed him, and as he paused at the bank of the dried riverbed, his eye caught something in the loose gravel. He was only thirty feet away now. He squatted down, precisely as he had done in the rehearsals. The light fell full upon him. He withdrew the shaped stone from the gravel, holding it carefully, turning it over in his hands. The scene was as I had visualized it weeks before. Then, through the viewer, I could see that he was still chewing furiously at the stick of gum.

With the camera still running I called out to him to stop chewing. "Yes," he replied, and his moving jaw continued without breaking rhythm. I called again. His reply was the same, and still he continued chewing. My third plea was as ineffectual as the first two. I stopped the camera. Rob had come jogging up to where the old man squatted with the axe. "We've got a problem," I said, as I scrambled up the bank. Rob looked at the Maasai, and he in turn looked at both of us. He seemed pleased with his work. "It's that blasted gum," I said. "He won't stop chewing it." Again I turned to the Maasai. "Usiile." This time, I mimicked his jaw going up and down and shook my head in disapproval. He nodded his understanding and kept on chewing. It was hopeless.

By now the cloud bank that had been moving eastward was almost completely dissipated. The huge ball of the sun hung over the horizon, magnified and reddened by the earth's atmosphere. I looked across the distance in time and space that the old man had traversed in his walk. His journey had been a thread of continuity that tied together so much of human evolution. But there was another element of continuity that was equally important — and that was the sun itself. In that long journey through time, man's dependence on the unfailing energy of the sun was so implicit that sun and life were in fact synonymous. It was the myriad fruits of the sun's energy that had made his journey possible from the beginning.

I think it was in my effort to get around his gum chewing that I first had the idea of having him hold the sun in his hand. The sun's height above the horizon was perfect, but we had to work fast. "Rob," I said, "have the old fellow stand over there. I want his hand outstretched from his elbow and just about the waist level. Get him to hold his hand palm up and slightly cupped. That way I can catch the sun as if he were holding it."

The Maasai was as obliging as always. There was simply

not enough time to explain in detail what I wanted him to do. At best it would have been hard for him to understand.

Through the viewer, I could see precisely how far Rob would need to raise or lower the old man's hand or move it left or right to position it just beneath the sun. After my efforts to get him to stop chewing, he must have thought I was a bit daft. Now he must have been certain of it. From where he stood, he could not possibly see the relation of his hand to the sun and the camera. One person was telling him to stand still. Another was forming his palm and fingers into a cup and moving it this way and that. He stood there looking at his hand and the ground beneath it. "Perfect! Great! Hold still just a minute," I called out — all meaningless phrases to him — in my frantic race against a moment that I knew couldn't last.

The old man was just visible in the darkness of the right side of the viewer, and although his jaw worked relentlessly in its contest with the chewing gum, it was hardly noticeable. We'd reached a compromise.

The huge star rested perfectly in his outstretched hand. Rapidly I checked again the waning level of light. Then I started the camera. Our timing had been perfect, but it had been completely a matter of chance.

The image in the viewer remains indelibly fixed in my mind. Once again I was peering into the time machine. Man held in his hand the gift of fire. It was a fearsome power that was to be both curse and blessing. With it he could fight the darkness or drive the hunted animal from hiding. He could clear the forest for planting and burn the grasslands before the yearly rains. In time it would become in other forms the welder's torch or the flame-thrower — and ultimately the blinding flash of the hydrogen bomb itself, mimicking in its terrible force the furnace of the sun.

The edge of the sun dipped below the horizon. I stopped the camera. A chill wind was beginning to rise. There would be no more filming that day.

We started to gather up our equipment. The axes were covered again in their cloth wrapping; their usefulness that day had been somewhat doubtful. I felt sorry that Richard's efforts on our behalf had gone to waste. That a stick of chewing gum and not the hand-axes had shaped the day's events was as much beyond our control as the fact that the sunset had been glorious.

Silently the four of us walked in darkness back to the car. The custodian of the site was waiting for us. We thanked him, said goodbye, and told him that we would take the Maasai back to his *manyatta*.

I climbed into the back seat with the old man, and we talked quietly as the car bumped along the dusty track. He directed Rob to the turning that took us to his house. In the headlights, we could see his wife waiting outside, a small child supported on her hip. Before the old man got out, I paid him for his help. There was much handshaking. He stood next to his wife, obviously proud of his family.

Several more of his children had gathered around us. Suddenly he reached inside his mouth, withdrew the infamous piece of gum, and as quickly placed it in his wife's mouth. It was like the passing of the baton from one runner to another in a relay. She entered wholeheartedly into the contest, working her jaw as hard as his had done.

As I looked at her, it came to me that the old man had not at all misunderstood my entreaties to stop chewing. I had told him in Swahili not to "eat" the gum. Obviously he had no intention of doing that; he had far better uses for it. Each time he'd nodded in agreement and persisted in his chewing. "Chew" and "eat" in Swahili as in English have distinct meanings. Events might have turned out differently that day had I known the Swahili for "chew". But then the old man might never have held the sun in his hand.

Of Ships, Giraffes, and Unicorns

Some years ago, I was walking the wave edge of a white beach on the East African coast of Kenya. It was early morning, and in the dim light I could just see the foaming line of surf far out along the barrier reef, the distant thunder of the waves reaching my ears long after I saw them curl and fall.

As the warm water swirled about my ankles and withdrew, I could feel the sand washing away from under my bare feet. Then I felt something small and hard, thicker than a seashell fragment and smoother than coral. Bending to pick it up, I saw it was a piece of pottery, its glaze a soft gray-green, and beneath the glaze a delicate pattern of what might have been part of a vine or even a piece of script.

I tucked it into a shirt pocket. For good luck? For the coincidence of finding it there? I don't really know why. I never saw it again.

Some months later, my work took me to Dar es Salaam, the capital of the neighboring country of Tanzania. Late one afternoon, I stopped to see an acquaintance of mine who worked at the King George V National Museum, as it was then called.

Since he was busy when I arrived, I wandered about looking at various exhibits of East Africa's past — skull fragments of early hominids from the digs of Louis and Mary Leakey, bones of prehistoric animals, and a myriad of artifacts from centuries of Arab trade followed by the brief influence of the Portuguese along the coast.

Then quite unexpectedly I found myself looking at something familiar — pieces of gray-green pottery with a delicate script-like pattern. The label on the case stated simply: Southern Sung Dynasty Chinese celadon ware, mid-13th century, site: Songo Mnara Island, Tanzanian coast.

How, I wondered, did pieces of the 13th-century Chinese pottery get to East Africa, and when? This wasn't part of any history I'd learned. I thought it was Vasco da Gama who'd discovered East Africa in the late 1400s by sailing around the Cape of Good Hope on his way to India. That da Gama and his ships accomplished this remarkable voyage was the result, as I understood it, of Portuguese superiority in navigation and shipbuilding. But then how could one explain the presence of Chinese artifacts from a period two centuries prior to the arrival of the Portuguese?

I was in the midst of all sorts of unanswered questions when my friend emerged from his office to find me bent over the pottery exhibit oblivious to his apologies.

After two hours and many cups of tea, I left his office carrying with me several borrowed books and a totally different perspective on history.

From the 7th century until the middle of the 15th, Chinese seafaring skills and shipbuilding technology were superior to those of any nation in the world. This little known part of Chinese history culminated in the Ming Dynasty (1368–1644) with seven extraordinary voyages between the years 1405 and 1433, the fifth and sixth of which reached the coast of Kenya. The purpose, at least in part, of the fifth voyage, 1417–19, was to return from a visit to China the ambassadors of Malindi (a prominent trading port on Kenya's coast) who had traveled to Peking three years earlier, taking with them a giraffe as a present for the Ming emperor. On one of these two voyages, the Chinese fleet reportedly consisted of more than sixty ships, including a hospital ship, a contingent of armed cavalry, and a special craft designed to carry sufficient fresh water for the Chinese personnel, whose number is estimated to have been a minimum of 27,000.

The books I'd borrowed revealed that the origins of Chinese long-distance maritime exploration and trade may have dated as far back as the 2nd and 3rd centuries A.D. to the time of the Han Dynasty. The French historian Pelliot believes that Chinese ships of that period were sailing as far as the Persian Gulf. While there is no historical evidence for such voyages, it is clear that Han Dynasty sailors were reaching ports throughout much of the Indian Ocean.

By the year 600 A.D., Chinese records tell of a naval architect named Yang Su who was building ships of five decks that measured 100 feet from the top of the mainmast to the keel. Such development soon led to a flourishing maritime trade for China during the Tang Dynasty (618–906).

It was during the subsequent Sung Dynasties (960–1279 A.D.) that the Chinese adapted the magnetic compass for use at sea 100 years before its appearance in the Mediterranean. So by the 12th century, Chinese ships, with their watertight bulkheads, their stern-post rudders, and their ability to sail into the wind, could travel, as one writer expressed it "wherever sailing ships could go, then or later."

Along with this growth in maritime skills came an increase in trade. In turn, this ignited amongst the wealthy court class a desire for such items as pearls, tortoise shell, ivory, rhinoceros horn, camphor, and frankincense. So great was this desire for foreign goods that by Sung Dynasty times there was a growing alarm at court over the shortage of precious metals brought about by the export of gold and silver coinage to pay for goods overseas. Consequently, under threat of execution, Chinese ship captains were forbidden to use any coinage for overseas trade. Instead, they were required to barter with Chinese porcelain, silk, lacquer-ware, and brocade. So when, in the 15th century, the Portuguese arrived at East African ports, to their surprise they found the handsome houses of wealthy

Arab merchants filled with exquisite Chinese products. The most durable of these was, of course, the porcelain, and it is said that today there are far more fragments of Sung and Ming Dynasty china along the East Africa coast than anywhere else in the world.

The seven great voyages that took place during the early part of the Ming period were under the direction of a Chinese admiral named Cheng Ho. It was he who led the expeditions to East Africa in 1417 and again in 1421. Cheng Ho was a member of the powerful eunuch class in the Ming court who had for centuries developed, planned, and carried out China's overseas exploration and trade.

The details of Cheng Ho's seven voyages were preserved in a remarkable stone inscription found in Fukien province in China in the 1930s. The stone had been erected by Cheng Ho and his companions in the year 1431 just before they set sail on their last voyage. On it were listed the dates of the previous expeditions and their expression of thanks to the goddess of the local temple for bringing them home safely so many times. On one part of the stone Cheng Ho wrote: "We have traversed more than one hundred thousand *li* of immense water spaces, and have beheld in the ocean huge waves like mountains rising sky-high, and we have set eyes on barbarian regions far away hidden in a blue transparency of light vapors, while our sails, loftily unfurled like clouds, day and night continued their course. . . ."

The eunuchs of the Ming court and their prosperous sea

trade gradually came into disfavor. There had always been a strong court faction that disapproved of Chinese contact with the outside world. Despite the obvious economic benefits they gleaned from the heavy taxes levied on imported goods, they shared in the Confucian belief that trade was an inferior profession, particularly one that dealt primarily with exotic luxuries. In time, this attitude gained control at court: the eunuch sea-traders fell from power; their ships, along with the records of their expeditions, were destroyed; and the great fleets sailed no more.

One fascinating sidelight of this unusual history concerns the giraffe that in 1414 was brought as a gift by the ambassadors from Malindi to the Ming emperor in Peking. It is reported that a year earlier a giraffe had been sent to China as a present from the new king of the country of Bengal in India. This king, at the time of his coronation, had received more than one giraffe as a gift from the emissaries of African countries who were guests at the ceremony. Perhaps it was to show his good intentions toward his distant neighbor, China, that he sent one of the giraffes to the Ming emperor. Knowing how pleased the emperor would be with the gift, the Chinese representatives at the Bengal coronation urged the African ambassadors from Malindi, who were also present, to come to China the following year to present another giraffe to the emperor. According to the Dutch historian J. J. L. Duyvendak, it was the special significance of this giraffe that may have prompted Cheng

Ho to sail all the way to East Africa in 1417 in order to see those ambassadors safely home.

But why should the giraffe be so special to the Chinese? Duyvendak suggests that the Somalis of East Africa, with whom the Chinese had traded, called the giraffe "girin". He says that the Chinese would have heard this word as "ki-lin" — a sound that would have been very close to "k'i-lin", their word for "unicorn". In Chinese mythology, the unicorn represented an aberration of nature that, along with dragons, could come into being only when there was a surplus of beneficent cosmic forces. Such a surplus could only occur during the perfect reign of a perfect emperor. So what better gift to curry favor than a unicorn for their emperor — a gift made possible by the eunuch merchants of China whose tide of power at the Ming court was already beginning to ebb?

Worlds Apart

There were no other aircraft ahead of us waiting to take off as we bumped over the grass and onto the tarmac of the small airstrip. Over the radio, a static-blurred African voice from the control tower at Wilson Airport gave us clearance, and without pausing we headed down the runway. The little Cessna rose easily into the air, leaving the dark silhouettes of the Ngong Hills on our left. Below us as we climbed over Nairobi National Park I saw a small herd of impala and near them a cluster of six giraffe, their long necks floating among the branches of the acacia trees on which they browsed. I had the distinct impression that we were beginning a flight into another time.

Looking behind us, I could see the sharp urban skyline of Nairobi disappearing slowly over the horizon, silhouetted now like a black paper cutout against a steel-gray sky. I settled back into one of the two rear seats and shifted the briefcase on my knees. Early that morning at the hotel, I had emptied it of papers and put in a small tape recorder, a pre-recorded cassette, a 35mm camera, an envelope of money, and a small packet of photographs. Whether I'd have any use for those things depended now entirely on luck.

The small plane with its pilot and two passengers turned southward toward the Tanzanian border. Our destination was a Dutch mission somewhere in southern Kenya near a place called Ilkerin. Two days before, I had spoken with the mission by radio-telephone from Nairobi and had been told that they had a useable landing strip. If we could put the plane down there, my plan was to continue south on foot or by a four-wheel drive vehicle if one were available. The mission had said that their only Land Rover was away for repairs, and they didn't know when it would be back. I had no choice but to gamble on its being back when we arrived.

Thus began my quest for an elderly Maasai woman whom I had never met. As the Maasai are a nomadic, pastoral people, all I knew of her whereabouts was that she might be in an area of southern Kenya and northern Tanzania that I had laid out on a map as fifty miles wide and about sixty miles long. Now I had only one day in which to try to find her in those 3,000 square miles, and as I watched the first raindrops make tiny tracks down the plane's windshield, I didn't think the odds for success were very good.

Mine was a purely personal quest. I could trace its beginning back sixteen years to the time when I had been working as education officer for the Tanzania National Parks. I had planned to make a film in Swahili for local African audiences telling the story of three secondary school students visiting one of the country's national parks, and my decision had been to pick a student from each of the major schools in the area near the park.

That was how I first met Onesmo oleMoiyoi. At that time, he had been the equivalent of an American eleventh grade high-school student in a Lutheran mission school hundreds of miles from his Maasai home in northern Tanzania. When I had asked the headmaster if he could single out his best scholar, athlete, and citizen all rolled into one, he had unhesitatingly called Onesmo into his office. Thus began a long and unusual friendship.

In time, Onesmo came to understand so clearly what I was trying to convey in the film that I asked him to read the Swahili narration. It was his knowledge of the local people and his skill with language that were primarily responsible for the film's widespread popularity. So much so that I asked him to do another film with me.

In the summer of 1962, with a grant from the New York Zoological Society, I invited Onesmo to come to the United States. My purpose was to make a film about his visiting Yellowstone National Park, America's largest and the world's first such protected area. I felt that a story, narrated by him in Swahili, might help African audiences to appreciate by comparison the unique wildlife resources of their own countries, and at the same time offer them a very different view of America than most Africans had.

During that trip to the United States in '62 I had arranged for Onesmo to visit Harvard University to take part in a summer training program for a small group of American college students who were preparing to go to Tanzania to teach. He was to serve as a Swahili language consultant for two weeks.

It was during this experience at Harvard that he decided that one day he would like to return there as a student. In the early '60s, many young Africans had such dreams.

His was a dream that came true, however. A year later he did in fact enter Harvard as a freshman on a full scholarship. In 1968 he graduated with honors and was accepted at Harvard Medical School. I continued to keep in touch with him over the years, during his internship and residency in Boston, and during his years of research in immunology at the Robert Bent Brigham Hospital. He often sent me copies of papers he had written for medical journals or was presenting at international conferences, and I sensed the growing recognition by the medical community for his outstanding work.

A few weeks before my trip to Africa, I had called him in Boston. "I'm going back to Kenya soon," I said, "and I thought I might be able to find your mother."

For a moment there was silence on the other end of the line. Then he said quietly, "That would be a miracle. I haven't seen her for years. A friend wrote that he'd heard she was in southern Kenya, twenty or thirty miles from a place called Ilkerin, but that was two years ago. I have no idea where she is now. Perhaps," he added, "Dr. Schaffer might know where she could be found. I believe he's still in Nairobi."

Roy Schaffer, an American doctor who had worked among the Maasai for thirty years and whose parents had been missionaries to the Maasai in Tanzania before that, was an old friend to both of us. In Kenya, it took me several days and innumerable phone calls until finally I located him through the Nairobi University Medical School where he was teaching. It had been fourteen years since we'd last met.

I was surprised at how unchanged he seemed. He was a short compact man, but at fifty still very trim. Unlike many Europeans in Africa, he was clean shaven. What I had remembered most vividly about him were his piercing dark eyes, bright with energy and intelligence. Over lunch Roy told me that he'd come across Onesmo's mother the year before. He had gone to the Ilkerin Mission and perhaps thirty miles south, near the Tanzanian border, he'd found her living with her people. She had been old and frail, walking with the help of a stick, he said, but she had seemed well.

"I told Onesmo I'd try to find her," I said. "Do you have the time to go with me?"

"Today's Monday," Roy reflected briefly. "I could go on Thursday, but after that I'm tied up."

On Tuesday, I was able to get Dr. Michael Norton-Griffiths to agree to fly us on Thursday to Ilkerin in his small research plane. A British research zoologist with his own wildlife consulting firm in Nairobi, Mike had been in East Africa for several years in charge of the aerial monitoring of the wildlife herds in the Serengeti National Park in Tanzania. Requiring a plane with rather unusual equipment for this work, he had flown out to Kenya from England in a specially outfitted single-engine Cessna.

Roy Schaffer now sat beside Mike in the front of the aircraft, while I sat behind them.

From the plane window, I watched as the land below gradually rose to parallel our slow climb. The altimeter read over 7,000 feet although the forest was only 500 feet below us. Then without warning we were seemingly hurtled upward into space as the land fell away 2,000 vertical feet, and we crossed the eastern edge of the Great Rift Valley.

We crossed the Ewaso Nyiro River. It lay on the earth like a giant python, its sluggish brown body dappled by occasional spots of sunlight breaking through the clouds. Ahead of us the sky was black. The huge Enguruman Escarpment that forms the west wall of the Rift Valley loomed darker still, its highest peaks hidden by clouds. We were headed into rain.

Below us now the deep gorges of the escarpment were covered in heavy forest. No roads there. Just dense forest filled with elephant and buffalo. Occasionally we could see a high waterfall drifting in white slow-motion over a rock face.

From the top of the escarpment the land continued to rise gradually to the southwest. At this point, Roy began looking for familiar landmarks. The first definite indication of where we were was the dirt track from Narok to Morijo. Ahead we could see the dark shapes of the Loita Hills. Somewhere out there to the south of those hills lay the small cluster of mission buildings.

Although we had climbed to 8,000 feet to clear the escarpment, we were still only 300 feet above the ground. The heavy cloud cover was beginning to break up as we entered a land of rolling hills that were endless replicas of each other. Then Roy pointed to one distant hill that held on its shoulder a distinctive single boulder the size of a house. There, on the southern slope, lay the mission buildings seemingly clustered together for company and protection against the vastness of the African bush, their tin roofs made startlingly bright by the broken patches of sunlight that turned the surrounding land yellow and green. As we circled low over the buildings, we could see a few cows and goats scared by the sound of the aircraft and some Maasai children waving and starting to run toward us.

We bounced down with a muffled thud on the makeshift grass strip that showed no sign of the wheels of recent aircraft. As Mike spun the plane around at the end of the strip and taxied back toward the buildings, we saw from behind the group of chattering children the Dutch missionary walking toward us. He was tall and very thin, dressed in a khaki bush shirt, his wavy blonde hair slicked to one side. He greeted us with a warm smile and, in broken but able English, explained that the mission's four-wheel drive vehicle had returned from Narok just that morning with a new set of tires. We were welcome to use it. Since there was no one at the mission who knew Onesmo's mother, our only hope of finding her, he said, would be to drive south to a Maasai village called Olpusimuru where someone might be able to help us. It had been only a short distance from that village that Roy Schaffer had seen her the previous year.

The missionary led us to a small dispensary to introduce us to Maria. She would drive us in the mission vehicle to Olpusimuru. Maria, a twenty-three-year-old Austrian nurse who had joined the mission three years before, had taken the Maasai to her ample, no-nonsense bosom and had mothered them through birth, illness, and death with a combination of caring and practicality that had earned both their affection and respect. She was known to them as "Maria oleDispensary". Every two weeks, she would take the mission's mobile medical unit into the surrounding miles of bush country to treat an incredible spectrum of ailments ranging from malaria to burns from the venom of a spitting cobra. She stood before us in the doorway of the dispensary kitchen wiping her wet hands on her apron, a red bandana covering her short brown hair, and a warm open smile on her red, freckled face. She was ready to go when we were.

Over a welcome cup of tea we estimated that it would take us almost another four hours to get to Olpusimuru, find Onesmo's mother, if possible, and return to the mission. Mike Norton-Griffiths elected to remain behind to catch up on some paperwork, but he was emphatic that we must get back to Nairobi before dark since the Cessna lacked the necessary instruments for flying at night. It was then only eleven o'clock, so we thought there was plenty of time.

The dirt track that led south toward Olpusimuru ran past the outbuildings of the mission and across a treeless plateau that stretched for miles in every direction. Two wheel ruts in the short grass marked the track, although in country like this, one could drive at will in virtually any direction — and easily become lost in an emptiness that offered no references by which to judge distance. Small herds of forty or fifty Thomson's gazelle watched us pass, their short black tails flickering across white rumps. There were wildebeest and zebra, as well as fawn-colored impala, and occasionally a large herd of Maasai cattle, their young warrior guardians silhouetted with their long spears against the skyline.

Gradually we dropped down the southern side of the plateau and entered a country of boulders and thorn trees stretching as far as the eye could see. We passed through several dry riverbeds, and once, as we emerged from a particularly deep gully, we found ourselves face to face with a herd of about thirty buffalo. Sunlight flashed from the black boss of their horns. Their shiny, blunt noses tested the wind, and then, with a burst of air from their nostrils, as if they didn't like what they smelled, they turned as one and vanished into the bush.

It took us an hour and a half to reach the few tin-roofed shacks that made up Olpusimuru. The main building was a small store known as a *duka* in Swahili. Fifteen or twenty Maasai, men and women of varying ages, were gathered at the *duka* entrance. They recognized the mission vehicle and greeted Maria with obvious pleasure. Once out of the vehicle, she walked to where three elderly women were seated on the ground. She bowed low before them, and they in turn touched the top of her head with their hands in blessing, as they would do with their own children.

Then began a long conference. Roy and Maria contributed, as did each of the bystanders. Because there was purpose to our visit, the local people became much involved, each offering an opinion. People began pointing in opposite directions. Some young women, dressed in heavily beaded cowskins and wearing silver bracelets, their legs wrapped to the knees in tight coils of bright wire, stood shyly to one side and listened. An old man with cataracts clouding both his eyes stared vacantly ahead. When he spoke, his voice was almost inaudible. Apparently he knew Onesmo's mother and explained that she had moved away from the place where Roy had seen her the previous year. The question was where and how far.

To ask directions of an African in the bush is one thing, but to ask how far is quite another. In Swahili the answer is always *mbali kidogo*. It means literally "just a little way — not far at all". What it really means is anywhere from one to fifty miles, and most likely closer to fifty.

One Maasai, taller than the rest, wrapped in an old blanket and little else, came out of the *duka*. He was carrying a tin of liquid margarine with a hole punctured in its top. As he listened and commented, he took long drinks from the yellow and blue can.

At first, the talk had included everyone. Gradually, however, people drifted off until only four or five remained. Suddenly the talk stopped. Roy turned to me and smiled. It was all settled. The man with the can of margarine was going to guide us to Onesmo's mother. It was *mbali kidogo*. This had taken three-quarters of an hour to decide.

"Where is the Kenya-Tanzania border from here?" I asked, through Roy.

"Beyond that hill. *Mbali kidogo*," Roy interpreted the answer of our self-appointed guide.

"The Maasai say there are no border guards anywhere near here," he added.

"Is Onesmo's mother in Kenya or Tanzania?" I asked.

"It doesn't make any difference," the man smiled, answering now in Swahili. "There are no roads through here anyway" — as if that somehow answered the question.

At first the vehicle followed wandering cattle tracks that threaded the dense thorn bush. As they gradually dwindled away, Roy and I walked ahead searching the undergrowth for rocks that might rip the oil pan from the bottom of the vehicle. As in attempting to negotiate a maze, we would find ourselves in a cul-de-sac of thorn trees. Either we would clear the way with *pangas* (the East African machete) or, if the trees were too big, we'd back out and search for a new route.

Finally we came out onto a ridge at the edge of a small valley. Our Maasai guide pointed across to the hills opposite. "The mother is there," he said.

As we dropped down into the valley along a dry streambed, we suddenly felt the vehicle lurch far over on its side. Climbing out, we saw that it was hung up on a small island of rock and sand, one of its rear wheels off the ground. Maria removed a shovel from behind the driver's seat and told us that if she were still stuck when we got back, then we could give her a hand.

Walking down the streambed carrying my briefcase, I felt like some salesman out of place and time — an anomaly in a world that had no need for any of the wares I might bring. Survival in this land depended on knowledge, not on things.

By now it was well after two o'clock. As we walked, I realized that it would be three or four hours more before we could possibly get back to the mission airstrip. If it began to get dark, I knew Mike would have to leave without us.

The sun was hot. Our guide, still clutching his can of margarine, stopped and pointed. There across the small valley, perhaps half a mile away, we could see a circle of thorn bush and a tiny plume of smoke.

We left the streambed and followed a cattle track that cut across the bottom of the valley. I had lost sight of the circle of thorn bush, and I was aware only of the silence surrounding the sound of our walking. I thought of Maria back at the truck attempting to dig it free; she'd been in Africa too long to be skittish about wildlife, but this was certainly rhino country and there were undoubtedly lion about.

We arrived at a clearing under a single large acacia tree whose canopy of shade made the air noticeably cooler. We stopped in front of the entrance to the high thorn enclosure called a *boma* in Swahili. Inside, the Maasai build their low houses of sticks and plastered cattle dung. At night, the cows and goats are herded inside the *boma* to protect them from predators. Our guide motioned us to wait while he went through an opening in the high wall. We saw and heard nothing, and I was surprised that there were no cows or goats anywhere.

In a few minutes he returned. Following him came an

old woman leaning on a long walking stick, and behind her came three young girls, like attendants on a noblewoman. She was tiny and wizened, but she carried herself with a kind of presence that came from age and undoubtedly from her own position in a family and clan. She walked toward us slowly but confidently. She stopped a few feet away and looked directly into my eyes. It was impossible to know what she thought as she saw me standing there with my briefcase. I greeted her in Maasai. We shook hands. Then Roy spoke to her, and perhaps she recognized him. It was difficult to tell. I kneeled on the ground, opened my briefcase, and took out a small packet of photographs in their waxpaper envelope. I handed them to the old woman, proffering them to her with both hands as is the Maasai custom, to show respect. One by one she examined each picture. She said nothing. Standing by her side I, too, looked at the pictures as she held them in her hands.

One of the photographs, taken at Harvard Medical School, showed Onesmo in shirt and tie and wearing the white coat of an intern. Another was of him in a tan L. L. Bean chamois-cloth shirt posed against an outcropping of rock on Mt. Monadnock in southern New Hampshire. Then there was a formal wedding picture of Onesmo and his white American wife Linda, and, finally, one of Linda alone in a spring garden standing partly sideways to the camera to show her long red hair reaching almost to her waist.

When I raised my eyes from the pictures, the old woman

was looking at me again. In the fine film of dust on her weathered face, I could see the shining tracks of tears. No one spoke. She looked again at each of the photographs, and then she uttered a deep sound from within, almost a cry, but there was pleasure in the sound beyond the sadness. She put the pictures carefully back in their small transparent envelope and held them in her hand tight against her breast. Then she looked at me once more — her eyes bright with tears and her cheeks still wet.

I asked if there might be a place where we could sit quietly out of the growing afternoon breeze to talk. We moved away only a few yards to the shelter of some piled thorn bush. Sitting on a fallen log, I opened my briefcase again and took out the small recorder. The cassette was already in place. I stood the recorder upright with its small speaker facing the old woman and pushed the play button. She was seated on the ground flanked by the three young women. None of them was prepared for what was about to happen.

Onesmo began to speak. As soon as his opening words of greeting were concluded, his mother answered him out loud. And as he continued to speak, she in turn responded.

As we sat there listening to his voice from so far away, I recalled him describing how he had made the tape late at night in a deserted laboratory in the hospital in Boston. I had called him just before I left the States for Kenya to say that I had received his packet of photographs, some money for his mother, and the tape cassette. To be sure that it would work properly, I had listened to it on the small recorder I planned to take with me. It had been a long time since I had heard those strange tonal inflections of the Maasai language, the musical intonations that are so hard for Westerners to imitate. Maasai is a Hamitic language, as different from the Bantu languages of East Africa as Chinese is from German. Roots of some Maasai words are believed to be traceable to ancient Hebrew origins.

"How long had it been since you'd spoken Maasai?" I had asked him on the phone. He laughed. "Too long," he said. "I had trouble with that tape. I had to go backward in time because I hadn't thought in Maasai for years, and when I finished the tape and was leaving the lab I ran into one of my colleagues in the corridor. To speak to him in English again, to make the shapes and sounds of English, required a whole change in viewpoint — a shift in personality."

The old woman, head bent forward, sat in the sun listening intently to her son's voice. In the heat, small beads of perspiration formed on the crown of her shaven head. From one of her long ear lobes, pierced and intentionally distended in childhood until now it reached her shoulder, there hung a single loop of colored beads. She was seated on the ground, her bare legs and feet stretched before her. Around one ankle there was a simple circle of wire. Along the edge of the cowskins she wore, there ran a delicate trim of colored beads. The thinness of her bare arms and shoulders made her seem very frail.

As Onesmo spoke to her, I looked beyond our small group to the tree-covered hills that formed the valley. I thought of these people whose days were shaped by the endless cycles of nomadic life, of dry seasons and wet, of the birth of calves and children, and the death of the sick and old — a world in which the fate of the cattle dictated the fate of the people.

Twice while he had been an undergraduate at Harvard, Onesmo had the opportunity to return to his home in Tanzania. On each occasion he had first traveled south from Nairobi to Arusha, the principal town in Tanzania's northern province, and there he would purchase a secondhand blanket and an old felt hat, changing into these from the Western clothes he wore. Then he would board a bus that would take him on a ten-hour ride across the miles of dirt track that led west and north to the tiny village of Loliondo near the Kenya border. The top of the bus would be piled high with baskets of live chickens and gourds of soured milk. Always there would be the Maasai and the heavy musky smell of fire smoke that permeates the cowskins and blankets they wear. On each occasion, as he had descended from the bus at Loliondo, there had been someone from the family to meet him. Yet he had told no one of his coming.

For a while he would be home again — going with his stepbrothers into the forests or mountains with a goat to slaughter to celebrate his return. He would live with them as he had as a child, yet he felt no need to try to tell them of the incomprehensible world from which he had come. Then he would return to America, to Widener Library, and to the physics and biology laboratories of Harvard.

On one of these trips home he had gone by himself before dawn into the mountains east of Loliondo. He described how in the morning sun the thermals climb the steep ravines. Vultures, after bathing in a pool or stream, ride the rising currents of air to dry themselves in the early morning sun, hovering a few feet from the cliff's edge. It was to this place that he remembered coming as a child once a year with his family and other members of his clan. In the rising sun, they would stand together naked to bathe themselves in the billowing currents of air as a ritual act of cleansing and purification. To return to that place years later and to sit by himself and watch the sun rise over the distant hills was, as he expressed it, "just like listening to Mozart".

At other times, he had spoken of his childhood and of the stories told by his grandmother around the fire in the *boma* at night. She had remembered the coming of the first Europeans to that part of Tanzania, and she had explained to the fascinated children that the skin of the white man was not normal in color because he came from a home under the sea where the sun never reached.

Onesmo's voice on the recorder had stopped. Except for the flies that buzzed in the warm air, it was silent. The old woman remained seated on the ground holding the packet of photographs in her hand. I spoke to Roy.

"Would you ask her if she would speak into the box so that I can take her words back to him?"

Roy translated my request. The old woman nodded, and the young girls threw back their heads in laughter and clapped their hands. I turned over the tape, adjusted the recorder's volume, pushed the button, and nodded to her. She began to speak. She was so small and frail that it seemed impossible that it was she who spoke with such power. There was no hesitation, no self-consciousness, no searching for words. She leaned close to the microphone as though it were a tiny opening that led from this place of light through a darkness and distance beyond imagining. Somewhere at the other end Onesmo was waiting and listening. This was his mother, and she was talking to her son.

When she finished speaking, the silence surrounded us once more. I rose to my feet too hurriedly, conscious of the time, and in Swahili I thanked the old woman. Our hands touched once more, and her eyes met mine. There were no longer any tears. She said something in blessing to all of us. Then she turned, and, with the three girls following, she passed back through the entrance into the *boma*.

The remaining details of that journey are blended in my memory to form a world that now seems timeless, yet always, even today, dominated by the sense of urgency to get back to the airstrip.

We found that Maria had succeeded in freeing the vehicle, and by the time we arrived, she had it turned around and was waiting for us. Our guide, who had jettisoned his empty can of margarine somewhere in the bush, announced that we would return to Olpusimuru by a new and shorter route. It would, by coincidence, he said, pass by his own *boma* where he would like to be dropped off. Despite his repeated assurances, we doubted the new route would be shorter. Why, asked Maria, hadn't we come the shorter way to begin with? The Maasai laughed and shrugged his shoulders. Apparently he had simply wanted a ride — the longer the better.

Winding our way slowly through the endless maze of thorn trees, we came upon a single white stone five or six feet high — a marker for the then closed boundary between Tanzania and Kenya. Unknowingly we had driven and walked several miles into Tanzania and now found ourselves crossing back over the border into Kenya. The stones had been far enough apart and the forest thick enough that we hadn't seen them on our way south.

Our guide had been right. The new route was nearly half an hour shorter than the way we had come. After depositing him at his *boma*, and after much hand shaking and mutual congratulations, we headed toward Olpusimuru. Passing the *duka* we waved but did not stop. The same figures as in the morning stood in the dust by the flimsy porch; only their shadows had lengthened.

Gradually we left the winding cattle tracks, the rocks and thornbush, and started the long climb to the top of the plateau. By the time we reached the open, the soft light of a lower sun had turned the plains to gold. The distant mountains to the north were bathed in the same light. In front of them lay a series of treeless hills, and on top of one of them we could see the huge, lone rock that marked where the mission lay. It was now five o'clock.

Time and distance floated in suspension. The far hills and the great rock seemed to come no nearer, despite our movement toward them. Only as the light changed was one aware that time had passed.

In the late afternoon, the eternal animals were feeding again on the endless grass. The black side-stripes and white bellies of the Thomson's gazelles flashed more brightly now — struck broadside by the lowering sun. A herd of a dozen or so giraffe ambled slowly across the plain. Through the heat haze their dappled bodies shimmered like strange fish seen through the shallow waters of some tropical sea. Imperceptibly, the small herds of impala changed color, as did the distant hills, from brown to russet.

We reached the mission, the sun still just above the horizon. At the end of the airstrip, we could see its light reflected from the blurred disk of the plane's whirling propeller as Mike prepared for takeoff. Maria raced the vehicle across the grass to block the path of the plane, and we tumbled out of the Land Rover before it had stopped. There was no time to say anything appropriate. As I heard Mike ease off on the throttle, I gave Maria an envelope with some money to help pay for our use of the mission's truck and for any damage that might have been done. There were hasty good-byes and then we were in the plane. It was five minutes after six.

I was grateful for the noise of the plane's engine. It made conversation impossible. We were being snatched too rapidly from one world to another and there was no time to adjust.

As we rose from the ground, I could see the Maasai children from the mission running and waving once again. We climbed slowly to the north over open forest. The trunks of the tall trees, like the gnomons of giant sundials, cast long shadows across the golden grasses beneath. We passed over a forest glade, and there in the rapidly falling light, I could see the dark shapes of forty or fifty buffalo — ebony carvings by an ebony pool. Up in the air, the afterglow of the sun burnished the under surface of the aircraft's wing, but down below, even as I watched, the forest was darkening to night.

My Father's Desk

This morning as I sit here at this old and familiar maple desk that belonged to my father, I am aware of a sense of loss — something so far away now that words can't easily call it back. Because it seems to be of the past, I wonder if it could simply be my own youth of fifty or sixty years ago. I think not. It seems to be something very different, more like the loss of some passion or overwhelming love toward which one strives or climbs throughout an entire life.

The old desk with its folding front that always lies open reveals a row of wooden cubbyholes filled with the flotsam and jetsam of the past — a snapshot of a much loved dog, now long since dead, an expired passport from the '50s, old postcards, and a yellowed telegram sent to an address in Tanganyika more than forty years ago.

In the middle of the row of cubbies there is a small square door with a sunburst like a scallop shell carved in the maple. I know that inside are a box of staples, a roll of Scotch tape, and an empty, round, brass container to hold a roll of stamps. What else there is I cannot say without looking.

With the door closed, what lies inside are like memories. They remain in the dark until consciousness sheds light upon them as when the little door is opened. But although they are always there, I find that sometimes there are things that I had forgotten.

Today when I open that door I find myself looking into a swirling blue mist through which is gradually revealed a graveled driveway lined on either side with Jacaranda trees in bloom. At the far end of the drive stands the low structure of the forest officer's guesthouse at Supkhar. Its thickly thatched roof beetles over freshly whitewashed walls and deeply recessed windows, and it looks rather like an Elizabethan cottage from a travel brochure from another time.

Midway between me and the building there is a small, very dark skinned man squatting on the driveway, rhythmically swinging a broom of twigs in a slow arc. In this way he gathers the fallen Jacaranda blossoms into little piles of intense blue — much as if he were sweeping up fragments of the fallen Indian sky.

Beyond him, on the terrace in front of the guesthouse, a wooden deal table and several chairs have been set out by barefoot men in white dhotis. They have gone now, but I recognize the furniture that we will be using after the evening meal — when the heat of the day has spiraled upward into the soft night and the earth has cooled — and after the small, dark man has swept away all the soft pieces of the fallen sky.

As I pass, I give him greeting, and he drops the broom to raise his hands with palms together to his bowing forehead. I hear him speak slowly, giving the three syllables an equal emphasis, "Na-mas-kar".

I pass through the arched doorway of the guesthouse and close the heavy wooden door behind me. The sound echoes through the cool and dim interior. As my eyes begin to adjust to the lack of light, I smell the musty odor of old books that have not been opened for a long time.

I am standing in a central hall that doubles as a formal sitting room with couches and chairs placed round the walls. There are two rather stylized and garish paintings on one wall. The first is of a tiger crouched and snarling upward through tall grass at hunters aiming rifles from their high perches on the backs of elephants. The other is of a forest scene dappled in bright sunlight showing several elephants and their mahouts in a logging operation. On the opposite wall between two doors there is a large, yellowed map showing the surrounding area as it was before Independence when Kanha National Park was a forest reserve under British authority.

An open door leads from each side of the central hall into the adjacent bedrooms. The smooth cement floors inside have been polished by years of waxing and buffing by a servant who, wearing sheepskin slippers with the wool side out, dances over the floors in the dim light singing softly to himself. Afterward he unrolls the russet-colored carpets from Rajastan that had been placed to one side while he worked.

The deeply recessed windows, screened and glass-louvered, are covered in thin gauze curtains, muffling the sounds outside. The separation is complete — between outside heat and inside cool, between outside sounds and inside quiet.

Looking up into the dark rafters overhead, I see hanging from them a huge woven grass mat known as a punkah. It is perhaps four feet high and almost as wide as the room itself, leaving enough clearance on each end to allow the punkah to swing easily in a long arc over the bed. A long braided rope attached to the bottom edge passes over the carved four poster bed with its white mosquito gauze and runs through a pulley where the ceiling and the wall meet. The rope descends the whitewashed wall almost to the floor and there it passes through another pulley and out through a hole in the thick wall to an outside porch. There, through the warm Indian night, the punkah wallah would sit on a low wooden bench with one leg crossed over the other knee and the rope attached to his foot or toe. Thus the slow movement of his crossed leg would provide the motion for the huge fan hanging from the rafters inside, the sound of its motion like the breathing of some giant sleeping creature in the darkened house. In the cool of the night just before dawn, the punkah wallah himself would fall asleep.

The sitting room opens at its far end into a dining area where the table has been set for our arrival later in the day in time for dinner. Along the far wall stands a sideboard with three empty decanters in a straight line and a silver tray with glasses and a pitcher. A small white cloth with dark blue beads hanging from its edges holds the cloth in place over the pitcher's top.

To the sideboard's left is an open door that gives onto the outside kitchen. Through it comes the sweet smell from the coals of a wood fire. Along the right wall of the dining room stands a large glass-fronted bookcase with its doors closed and locked. On one glass door a piece of paper had long ago been taped, its lower edges curling upward now. There, carefully printed by hand and in English, is Robert Frost's poem "Stopping by the Woods on a Snowy Evening". Beside it is a copy of the poem translated into Hindi. Underneath the two versions is a drawing of a man standing in a forest. Beneath him is written the name "Jawaharlal Nehru" and under that, in the same hand, "December 1951 — Supkhar".

Behind the glass doors of this guesthouse "library" I can read some of the titles: *Marazan* and *So Disdained*, both early novels by Nevil Shute; a collection of poems by Rabindranath Tagore; and on the lowest shelves are tattered piles of old *Blackwood's* magazines, the top one dated April 1921. There are books whose covers are missing from use, mysteries probably, and I can just make out a battered copy of Kipling's *Plain Tales from the Hills*. There are others whose titles I can't read.

On top of the bookcase are ten or more large record books, chronologically ordered beginning in 1903 and forming a diary of events from the surrounding forest reserve as kept by the various chief forest officers over the period of some forty-four years before India received her independence and Kanha became a national park. Tonight in this room we shall eat dinner by the light of candles and kerosene lamps, and we shall talk of the India of another time — of tiger hunting, and of training wild elephants, and of the ritual worship of cobras by the local Gond tribe.

After dinner, we move outdoors for coffee on the gravel terrace in front of the guesthouse where the deal table and several chairs have been placed for our use. There in the moonlight, the once carefully swept terrace is covered again now in fallen Jacaranda blossoms. They seem in this soft light like a dusting of black snow.

Apart from my two American colleagues there are four Indians: Jagat Dutta, Chief Wildlife Warden for the state of Madhya Pradesh; Himu Panwar, Warden of Kanha National Park; Parihar, Director of Project Tiger in Kanha Park; and Kotwal, the Chief Research Officer. All are men whose entire professional lives had been dedicated to conservation work. Two of them are graduates of the prestigious Indian Forestry School at Dehra Dun, and the other two have come up through the ranks as wildlife and forestry field officers.

The preservation of traditions of service along with an intense sense of pride in their accomplishments are as important to them as they were to their British predecessors.

Over glasses of Indian Scotch and warm, boiled water we talk of their success in tracking the park tigers with radio collars. There are now in the park seventy-one tigers in all — a figure made possible they say only because the local villagers have been rewarded for contacting the police if a marauding tiger should attack their cattle. The police notify the park by radio, and a team arrives by truck at some abandoned village hut into which the tiger has been driven by people banging on pots and pans. The tiger is darted through a window with a sedative and transported into the park where it is collared with a radio transmitter and placed in the custody of a game scout for several weeks until it has been assimilated into the life of the park. The game scout's primary responsibility is to see that the tiger stays within the park boundaries — which means that, if necessary, he will shoot food for it. And the villager whose cow has been killed by a tiger outside the park will be compensated for his loss by the local government.

Our conversation stops abruptly. From just to the left of the guesthouse comes a series of deep grunts of a hunting tiger. It is followed immediately by others to the right, neither as deep nor as long — a female. And then further to our right a third one — another female. We sit poised, our breathing suspended, waiting. Again the male grunts several times, and I can hear the intake of each breath. He can't be more than seventy-five feet to our left just behind the guesthouse. A female answers him from the gravel drive. The other calls from further away now. They are on a hunt, passing through and around us.

As their sounds grow fainter, Panwar speaks softly. "In the bookcase in the dining room," he says, "the old records report that the last time tigers were heard at the Supkhar guesthouse was in May of 1914. We've been waiting all those years for this night. So they are making a comeback and we know our work is bearing fruit."

In my mind's eye, in the dim light of the moon I see a huge soft foot, its claws retracted, silently crushing the fallen blossoms of the Jacaranda trees on the gravel drive.

And I close the little door in my father's desk.

This book has been set in Galliard type, a design by Matthew Carter based upon the sixteenth-century designs of Parisian typecutter Robert Granjon. The text ornament is a Hermann Zapf design. The book was printed at The Stinehour Press in Lunenburg, Vermont, on 80-pound Mohawk Cream Vellum paper. Design is by Avanda Peters of Stinehour Design. The book was finished at Acme Bookbinding, Charlestown, Massachusetts.